MEANINGFUL WORK

NINA MAPSON BONE

MEANINGFUL
WORK

Unlock your unique path
to career fulfilment

PRAISE FOR *MEANINGFUL WORK*

'Nina has written a book I didn't know I needed to read – it's an essential guide to getting more out of your working life, and building happy, effective and motivated teams. It's free of jargon, and packed with useful tools to help you make better decisions during a time of profound change in the world of work.'

Liz Gibbons, Executive Editor, BBC World Service

'Work. The vast majority of us have to do it, and we will spend one third of our life doing it. However, for an activity we will spend a significant amount of our time doing, most do not find it fulfilling or meaningful. Through theory, exercises, and personal stories, *Meaningful Work* takes you on a journey to discover the meaning in your work, and should you not find it, guides you through the steps to ensure your next role is a meaningful one.'

Zrinka Lovrencic, CEO, WRK+, Compiler of 'Best Places to Work' List

'With practical insights, personal experience and backed by credible research, this book provides everyone with a new way of looking at ourselves at work. It stimulates self-reflection and helps create a path for more meaning. This is such a powerful book for the modern world of work by an author who lives and breathes the topic with unmatched passion. A must read!'

Daniel Murray, CEO, Empathic Consulting

'Let's face it, we've all had that moment in our working lives where we've asked ourselves, "What's this all for?" Meaning is the currency of happiness for many and *Meaningful Work* not only provides a methodology for finding this gold but, most importantly, provides super-practical guidance on how to ensure that we retain it. Whether you're a leader, a doer, a thinker or something else altogether, happiness, productivity and the pursuit of something bigger than ourselves is to be found in *Meaningful Work*.'

Charles Cameron, CEO, Recruitment, Consulting & Staffing Association of Australia and New Zealand

'*Meaningful Work* is refreshing, funny, genuinely inspiring and true to the title. For me, the individual stories are the highlights as they link real-life examples to the four factors of meaningful work. Nina has been able to articulate something that people feel and know is there but are unable to bring it all into one place. I really loved it.'

Zoran Jurisic, Head of QuickBiz and Digital Acquisition, NAB

'This book is an invaluable contribution to individuals … with far-reaching consequences for the wider communities that bear the consequences of disengagement in the workplace and our economy … If you seek clarity on what meaningful work means for you, this book delivers. You now possess the key to aligning your career and work choices with your life at this very moment. What an invaluable gift that is.'

Carolyn Butler-Madden, Chief Purpose Activist, Speaker, Author

'Regardless of your stage of career or your phase of employment in your current role, consideration of how meaningful and therefore how satisfying, challenging, rewarding and fulfilling your work is to you is always worth investing time in considering. In this practical, easy-to-read book, Nina sets out a framework based on excellent research, with great examples and helpful self-reflective exercises. It is an excellent resource to carry with you throughout your career and use repeatedly, especially at times when considering a job transition.'

Anthony Sork, Managing Director, Sork HC
Owner of shcBOND Employee Attachment Inventory | Employee Connection Inventory | Employee Detachment Inventory

'Working in a sector that struggles with attracting and retaining the best possible candidates, the quest for ensuring that we offer meaningful work has never been more important. It's much more than offering purpose and impact, building the best culture requires multiple elements and this book provides a clear path and ideas on how we can all do that – whatever industry we work in. I wish it had been available when I first started leading teams!'

Helen Merrick, General Manager – Fundraising & Marketing, Mission Australia

'In *Meaningful Work*, Nina Mapson Bone leads us on a journey of exploration, challenging our conventional perspectives on work and its implications for personal growth and societal development. Each page bears testimony to her deep understanding of the human element of work in a world that is increasingly dominated by technology. Mapson Bone successfully captures the intrinsic value of work beyond the mere transactional, delving into the psychological, relational, emotional, and social dimensions that contribute to a truly meaningful experience. Her pragmatic yet compassionate approach blends the latest research, real-life narratives, and thought-provoking anecdotes. This book is not just for employees or employers but anyone who seeks to understand the integral role work plays in our lives and society.

Meaningful Work is a must-read for those yearning for a more holistic, fulfilling experience in their professional lives. It offers deep wisdom, practical strategies, and inspiring perspectives. Nina Mapson Bone has delivered a book that resonates with authenticity, wisdom, and insightful guidance.'

Michael Ellis, Head of People and Culture, Everyday Massive

For Paul and Callum, without whom
I wouldn't have meaningful work.

CONTENTS

FOREWORD

I first met Nina Mapson Bone when I started working with the leadership team of Beaumont People to help them uncover their organisational purpose and embed it into their strategy. It was 2018 and back then, meaningful work was often used as a vague expression by people to describe a generic need state.

In discovering Beaumont People's higher purpose, we revealed what was already there, hidden but nonetheless subconsciously driving the behaviour of the leaders and employees within the business.

Recognising meaningful work as their driving purpose, the next question begging for an answer was – what is meaningful work? A little research revealed that despite the frequent use of the term 'meaningful work', nobody had provided a practical definition or the means to help people find it.

I won't spoil the unfolding of this story. You can explore it in this book. However, I would like to highlight Nina's profound dedication to meaningful work. Like others motivated by a clear and unifying purpose, it has become her passion. This book is just one manifestation of her leadership in this significant movement.

If you're wondering why meaningful work matters, consider the current state of employee engagement in Australia and New Zealand, or rather, the lack thereof. Now, imagine the cost this incurs for workplaces and the broader economies.

People don't want to be disengaged. Most individuals seek a sense of meaning in their work. The problem arises when they lack clarity about what 'meaningful work' means to them. This lack of clarity leads individuals to pursue work they feel they 'should' do, whether it aligns with their parents' or society's expectations or their peer group's. Eventually, all too often, they find themselves unfulfilled, unhappy and trapped.

For those fortunate enough to have found meaningful work, the benefits extend well beyond the individual. Meaningful work has a profound ripple effect. A person who feels happy and fulfilled in their work positively influences their colleagues and employer. Their organisation reaps those rewards. When that person returns home, feeling valued and fulfilled in their work, they approach their family, friends and community with a positive attitude, instead of feeling unappreciated and unsatisfied, which may result in taking out frustrations on their family and withdrawing from social networks.

I don't think it is overreach to suggest that making meaningful work accessible to more people would lower the rate of stress and subsequent mental health issues in our communities.

That is precisely why this book is an invaluable contribution to individuals in the realm of work, with far-reaching consequences for the wider communities that bear the consequences of disengagement in the workplace and our economy.

Nina's passion for meaningful work radiates through her writing as she shares the valuable insights that Beaumont People has accumulated through their research over the last four years, as well as their work in recruitment and professional development. She breathes life into these insights by presenting captivating examples of individuals and their career choices. These case studies encompass people from diverse backgrounds, emphasising the factors that influenced meaningful work at different stages of their lives and careers.

Nina skilfully engages the reader by encouraging them to apply these insights to their own lives through thought-provoking questions and simple exercises.

As I read this book, I felt as though I were sitting down for coffee with Nina, listening attentively as she imparted crucial information. She eloquently simplifies complex concepts and enlivens them with engaging stories. Reading this book is truly a delightful experience, as Nina's special blend of passion, optimism and humour shines through her writing.

If you seek clarity on what meaningful work means for you, this book delivers. You now possess the key to aligning your career and work choices with your life at this very moment.

What an invaluable gift that is.

Carolyn Butler-Madden
Chief Purpose Activist, Speaker, Author

INTRODUCTION

Have you ever thought about a world where people everywhere are engaged in meaningful work?

Where not only are you happy and committed in work, but where everyone around you is too?

A world where your job allows you psychological safety?

Where you are fully engaged?

Where you can create, collaborate and contribute?

Where what you do makes a difference, where what you do *matters*?

This is a world I think about all the time.

Unfortunately, this is not the world we inhabit today. We are facing a meaningful work crisis.

According to Gallup's 'State of the Global Workplace: 2022 Report', job unhappiness is at a staggering all-time high, along with worker disengagement. These levels of unhappiness and disengagement are coinciding with workplace changes the likes of which we have never seen before. The shifting demographics of our population mean there will be a continued talent shortage in key areas over the coming years.

Artificial intelligence is also changing the nature of workplaces, and the types of skills we will need is evolving at an unprecedented pace.

You might be wondering what this means for you. You wouldn't be alone. With the decline of many traditional forms of community, work has taken on greater significance for our identity, purpose and meaning, and how we tackle these big issues matters at a personal level.

It's why we at Beaumont People commissioned our world-first research into meaningful work so we could truly understand the problem we were trying to solve. In reading this book you'll learn the three key messages that will help you understand what meaningful work actually is, you'll know the four factors of meaningful work, and you will have clarity on how the future of meaningful work is likely to unfold. You'll be given the tools to unlock your own unique path to meaningful work and gain an understanding that it can change over time.

You'll then be able to revisit those tools as often as you like so you can continue to tweak what meaningful work means for you as your circumstances change.

I hope you enjoy discovering the many ways in which work can become meaningful for you.

HOW TO USE THIS BOOK

The very best way to use this book is to read it cover to cover, in order, with a pen and notepad at the ready, undistracted and giving it your full attention. (You'll also find spaces throughout to take notes and respond to questions, but you'll still need the notebook.) Now, I'm a realist and expect that, oh, about, say, 5 per cent of readers will actually do that. If you're absolutely, definitely, never in a month of Sundays going to do that, jump to the next paragraph and I'll share the cheats' way of getting the best out of the book.

Here's why you should read it in order (and *ha!* you fell for it didn't you? If you want to cheat, you actually have to skip to the *next* paragraph). Finding and keeping meaningful work is a bit of a Holy Grail. It takes effort and persistence. The best chance you have is to arm yourself with as much information as possible, and the best way to do that is to read this book and understand the theory, be inspired by the real-life stories, do the exercises, and learn how work is likely to play out in the future. By actively participating in all four areas of the book you are more likely to see how they come together and therefore more likely to recognise how meaningful work affects you as an individual. You will notice when something has changed for you. You might pick up if there is a tension between two of the different factors for you and understand that only you can resolve that tension. You'll see work in an entirely different way and have a lot more influence on how you make it meaningful in the future.

However, if you struggle to read a book from start to finish, and I know plenty of people do, then absolutely use the book to help you in the way that will make it most meaningful for you. As a minimum, ensure you understand the three key messages and the four factors of meaningful work.

Outside of that, if you find real-life stories inspiring, go ahead and enjoy them. They have been hand-selected to provide you with a diverse range of people from different backgrounds, with different experiences of meaningful work. Some of them knew from a young age how they found meaning, others took a more winding route. My hope is that, no matter your personality or background, you might find someone who will inspire you within the stories. As you learn about the theory of meaningful work, you'll start to see how it has unfolded within these stories. You might then see parallels between some of their experiences and some of the challenges you have faced, even if their circumstances are different from your own. Each, in their own way, shows that there is a path to meaningful work, even when it may seem out of reach at times.

But if this isn't your thing … feel free to skip them.

If you find the research boring, skip it! If my talk of demographics and artificial intelligence in the future puts you off, please don't let that be the thing that stops you in your pursuit of meaningful work. Finally, if the exercises feel too much like being back at school, you can always just think about them rather than writing anything down.

In the end, it's up to you.

Okay, shall we then?

PART I
UNLOCKING YOUR UNIQUE PATH TO MEANINGFUL WORK

CHAPTER 1

WHAT IS MEANINGFUL WORK?

A quick Google search will provide you, in about half a second, with over a million links to pages referencing meaningful work. You've probably heard the term 'meaningful work' being bandied around … a lot. I have Google alerts set up to let me see any reference to the term that is being publicly shared, and I had to change the settings to only alert me once a day as it was constantly sending me notifications. It's a term that is regularly seen in the news, and not just the business news. Yes, there are articles in *Forbes*, *Fortune* and *Harvard Business Review*, but there are also regular articles in national news outlets too – from *Nine News* to ABC in Australia, through to *The Times* of London, *The Times* of India and *The New York Times*, to name just a few.

The quest for meaningful work is human and it is universal.[1] And with the quest for meaningful work comes the trend of new terms used to help describe the things people do, or don't do, to find meaningful work, such as 'quiet quitting', 'hybrid working' and 'start with why', or even, as an old boss once said to me, 'win their wallets and their hearts will follow'.

---

1   'Meaningful work and the development of a Meaningful Work Profiling Tool', Dr Jill Rathborne and Dr Elizabeth Shoesmith, November 2019.

At time of writing there is a shortage of critical talent. Unemployment in Australia is at record lows, and even though it will fluctuate with economic cycles, the long-term trend towards talent shortages will become more challenging, as we'll see in later chapters.

Work trends are regularly written about and commented on. The latest published research by Gartner shares nine high-impact trends which they promise will 'create an exciting opportunity for organisations to differentiate themselves as an employer of choice.'[2] In other words, an opportunity for organisations to create more meaningful work for their people.

As leaders we often struggle to attract, retain and develop quality employees. Yet, as workers ourselves, we also quietly wonder if our own role is meaningful. We question, if there is such a talent shortage out there, how could *I* find more meaning in my work?

These questions we ask ourselves are not unique. According to the *McKinsey Quarterly* Report 2022[3], meaningfulness of work was a top factor driving retention, as shown in the following chart.

So, we knew we were onto something when we started thinking about meaningful work.

---

2   www.gartner.com/smarterwithgartner/9-future-of-work-trends-post-covid-19
3   'The great attrition is making hiring harder. Are you searching the right talent pools?' Aaron De Smet, Bonnie Dowling, Bryan Hancock and Bill Schaninger. *McKinsey Quarterly*, 13 July 2022.

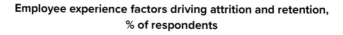

Employee experience factors driving attrition and retention, % of respondents

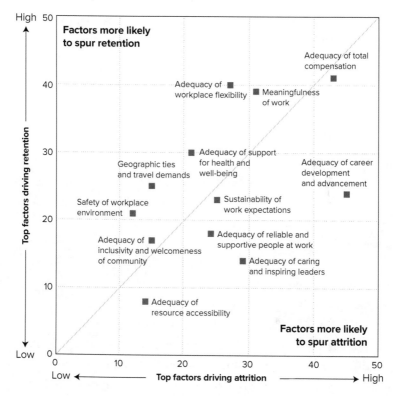

Data derived from: *McKinsey Quarterly* Report, 13 July 2022

UNCOVERING THE IMPORTANCE OF MEANINGFUL WORK

The story of how we came to uncover the importance of meaningful work starts, as every story does, with a couple of key characters. Nikki Beaumont, founder and CEO of Beaumont People, opened the business in 2002, after coming to Australia to run a significant recruitment project for the Sydney Olympics. She had a vision for a recruitment organisation that cared about its people, both internally as well as those it was placing. She wanted to establish a business that thought beyond the start date of a placement. She wanted to know how the people Beaumont People were placing were really contributing to the organisations they were working in; and how they, in turn, were getting deep satisfaction from their work within those organisations.

Nikki and I crossed paths formally in 2015. I say formally because before this point we knew each other through the industry. We knew each other to wave to across a room at a networking function, and in fact I had bumped into her once at the local Aldi, and unbeknownst to us at the time, our kids went to the same school. But we'd never sat down and had a coffee. We had never had an in-depth conversation.

So, when she rang me out of the blue one Sunday afternoon wanting to know if I was interested in exploring working with her, I was somewhat surprised. Surprised she had my number, surprised she was calling me on a Sunday. Surprised she knew enough about me to be asking if I wanted to work with her. Knowing what I know now, none of that is surprising! What is surprising now is, I said *no*.

But I was intrigued to get to know Nikki better and over time, as we discussed more, I saw in her, and in Beaumont People, something I hadn't seen in my career until that point. Something different. Nikki had always run the charity part of her recruitment business as a not-for-profit itself. By significantly reducing fees for the charity sector, she was giving back to those organisations so they could use their funds where they were most needed. Here was someone running a business in a completely different way.

This was incredibly inspiring to me. Since starting on this journey, I have learnt that, for me, meaningful work is about contributing to our communities and doing work that carries a higher purpose. I'd always felt that connection within my job roles, as there is something deeply satisfying about helping others find work. However, it was often missing at an organisational level. This doesn't mean the organisations

I had worked with previously weren't providing meaningful work, in other ways they absolutely were, and I have them to thank for my experience and career development. But they weren't providing work that was meaningful specifically to me. As you'll learn later, everyone's path to meaningful work is unique. There is no right or wrong.

I joined Beaumont People in 2015 and became a partner in the organisation a couple of years later. In the time that Nikki and I have worked together, we've been able to continue the journey she started, always thinking about how we could create more opportunities for meaningful work, both internally and externally. We were an industry first in launching a gender-neutral paid parental leave scheme in 2017, and we were one of the first organisations in Australia to implement a four-day work week, allowing our team to work four days while getting paid for five.

SO, WHAT *IS* MEANINGFUL WORK?

We define our purpose as:

> We exist to connect people to meaningful work and to create more opportunities for meaningful work in Australia.

To be true to this purpose we first needed to understand what meaningful work was. But when we investigated it, we were astounded to discover that there was no universal definition of meaningful work; there had never been any research done into what meaningful work is specifically for Australians; and there was no research anywhere in the world that combined both the psychological and sociological aspects of meaningful work (more on that later).

How could we create opportunities for meaningful work if we couldn't even describe how to attain it with any confidence? When I have asked people anecdotally about 'meaningful work' I tend to get responses to do with culture, or engagement, or perhaps leadership. When I dig deeper into why the person may think that, the answers tend to be vague or I get directed to studies that were specifically just about those topics in the first place. When a study is only looking at a limited number of factors of meaningful work it's hard to see the full picture. So, we decided to truly get to the bottom of what meaningful work is.

In 2019 we began some world-first research into what makes work meaningful. This was an Australian first in being the only such research done specifically for Australians, and a world first in being the first study to combine the psychological and sociological aspects of meaningful work. We were really proud that this report, 'Meaningful Work and the Development of a Meaningful Work Profiling Tool', was published in 2019 and is available to download on our meaningful work website.[4]

WHAT DOES ALL THIS MEAN FOR YOU?

It was through this research that we came up with a definition of meaningful work:

> Meaningful work is the importance an individual places on their work meeting their current personal beliefs, values, goals, expectations, and purpose in the context of their social and cultural environment.

In the next chapter, for those of you unlikely to read the academic paper (most of us, let's be honest!), I will share the findings of the research in detail with some inspiring true stories to bring it to life. But before I do, I'd love you to undertake a little exercise. This is an

---

4   www.meaningfulwork.com.au

exercise I get the audience and participants to do whenever I'm speaking on meaningful work, and it is a few simple questions:

1. What makes work meaningful to you?
2. What do you think are the three most popular factors of meaningful work?
3. Do you think what makes work meaningful over time can change?

Spend a moment thinking about these questions and jot down your answers below.

1. _____

_____

_____

2. _____

_____

_____

3. _____

_____

_____

Okay, let's see if what you said matches what the research found!

CHAPTER 2

WHAT THE RESEARCH SAYS

We concluded the previous chapter with our definition of what meaningful work is. Let's see how we came to that definition.

UNCOVERING THE GAPS IN EXISTING RESEARCH

The research we commissioned first reviewed what had already been published in this space. As you'd expect, there was a vast amount, but we discovered that there were some significant gaps. There was no consistent definition of meaningful work, no consistent techniques to measure it, and previous approaches had made explicit and restrictive assumptions.

The previous research applied definitions and measures of meaningful work that assume each factor's importance and assume that importance does not change over the course of an individual's lifetime. In layperson's terms, the previous research made assumptions about how important certain factors were, not recognising that the importance of those factors could change from person to person, and over time. So, for example, I might be very tied to money as a factor of meaningful work, but for you it may not be as important. Furthermore, I might be particularly motivated by money right now because I have a big mortgage I'm trying to pay off, but once I've put a dent in that mortgage the amount of money I earn may become less important and other factors may become more influential for meaning in my work. Yet, all the previous research in this area did not allow for such factors to change over the course of our lifetimes.

THE INTEGRATED APPROACH

What we did confirm through the research was the quest for meaning is an innate human need, and work has become one of the main ways we seek to fill that need. Our work provides an income to live and support ourselves and our families, but with the decline of traditional sources of community and social support, such as the decline in church attendance or the decline in knowing our neighbours, work has become a primary source of personal identity, significance and meaning. This rise in the importance of meaningful work was confirmed through our initial survey, with 71 per cent of people in 2019 believing that 'having meaningful work was more important today compared with five years ago'.

The other fascinating observation to come out of our research was that all the previous studies sat in one of two schools of thought:

- The first was that meaning in work is about ourselves as individuals; our experiences, beliefs, values and attitudes. This is known as the *psychological perspective*.
- The second school of thought is that the social and cultural systems around us assign value to our work activities. There has been less research into this *sociological perspective*, but it's an important consideration when defining and evaluating meaningful work. For example, how many of us who home-schooled our children during the pandemic changed our view of how meaningful teaching is as a profession?

Even if we didn't home-school children, we can look to the many different ways in which different countries celebrated their healthcare heroes during the pandemic to see how much value we assign to the health and medical profession from a cultural perspective.[5] Here in Australia, we had much of Melbourne's famous street art becoming focused on healthcare workers, and the southern hemisphere's largest billboard on the Anzac Bridge in Sydney was covered with hundreds of photos of healthcare workers with the words 'Thank you'. In Philadelphia in the United States 150 drones flew in coordination spelling out the words 'Thank U Heroes', and in the UK Captain Tom More, a World War II veteran who uses a walking frame, raised £29 million for the NHS by walking 100 laps of his garden, and London did the weekly 'clap for our carers' campaign with people standing at their doors and windows applauding the work of the healthcare professionals. These are all examples of how, culturally, we shifted the value we assign to work activities as a result of a sociological situation.

Another way to think about this is to consider how your own culture views the job of being a parent. It is very common for this role to be viewed quite differently depending on the lens you are looking through. In a lot of cultures, mothers are encouraged to be stay-at-home mums. It is well regarded, and as a mum you are often given significance within society if you are performing that role.[6] Yet in many of those same societies if the dad chooses to be the stay-at-home parent they can feel quite differently. The social structures of support are not there in the same way – there are more often 'mothers' group' and 'mums and bubs' classes. The questions and judgements a stay-at-home dad receives from his peer group are often very different to those a stay-at-home mum would get. An article from February 2023 quotes a stay-at-home dad

---

5   www.opencolleges.edu.au/blog/2020/06/24/different-countries-celebrating-their-healthcare-heroes/
6   *Heading Home: Motherhood, Work and the Failed Promise of Equality*. Dr Shani Ograd, 2019.

who tells people he's 'involved in start-ups' because he feels negative judgement, despite the fact he has a closer relationship with his teenage son and enabled his wife to pursue her master's degree.[7]

Negative social perceptions can colour how valuable a person feels their role is, even though everything about the job – the hours, the place of work, the child they are looking after – are exactly the same.

It was this gap in the research between the psychological and sociological perspectives that struck us. We intrinsically feel that meaningful work should be seen through both lenses, what we call the *integrated perspective*. This view understands that meaningful work is a complex relationship between the individual, the job, the organisation and the society and culture in which we live.

Diverse workplaces are better performing, but getting a diverse group of people to work together well is more difficult than for a group of people with similar backgrounds.[8]

When I first heard about the psychological and sociological perspectives it reminded me of the differences between individualism and collectivism among different cultures. There has been some significant research into the idea that people in Western cultures (such as the US, the UK, Europe) tend to be more individualistic and people from Eastern cultures (such as India, Japan, China) tend to be more collectivist.[9] This is not my area of expertise, but it is relevant here in terms of how it affects our approach to work from a sociological perspective.[10]

---

7   www.bbc.com/worklife/article/20230206-are-stay-at-home-dads-becoming-more-common
8   'Diversity wins: How inclusion matters.' McKinsey & Company, 19 May 2020.
9   Triandis H.C. & Suh E.M. 'Cultural influences on personality'. *Annual Review of Psychology.* 2002;53:133–160.
    www.ncbi.nlm.nih.gov/pmc/articles/PMC5761731/
    www.bbc.com/future/article/20170118-how-east-and-west-think-in-profoundly-different-ways
10 If you want to geek out there is some fascinating research into why there seem to be differences in individualism vs collectivism in different areas and cultures, with ideas beyond just history, geography and culture shaping our thinking. There is some evidence to suggest your social orientation can even change the way you see things, and there's even some suggestion that it can affect how likely you are to get an infection! See the references to find out more if you want to while away an evening going down an internet rabbit-hole.

In Australia, where workplaces have a healthy mix of people from Eastern and Western cultures,[11] it is important to understand that what makes work meaningful could be very broad ranging. As a recruiter, I learnt early in my career that putting my own assumptions of meaningful work onto the candidates I was trying to help was a sure way to place them in positions not right for them. To become good at my job I had to become better at asking questions that would help me understand their needs and wants more, and I had to get better at articulating that to others when it didn't necessarily match my own beliefs or values.

THE RESEARCH TELLS US ...

As a result of this research, we confirmed how important meaningful work is. Unsurprisingly, 98 per cent of the people we surveyed agreed that having meaningful work is important. We saw that having meaningful work increases job satisfaction, improves career development, creates less work stress and impacts positively on health and wellbeing. We also saw the positive impact for organisations. When your team members are enjoying meaningful work they have higher engagement levels, less sick leave, and are less likely to leave your organisation. Your people will have higher commitment to your organisation, and your overall organisational performance improves, even increasing your organisation's performance during times of downturns or downsizing.

The reasons finding meaningful work is so challenging for such a large number of people was jumping out at us as a result of our research. There is a lack of:

- clarity in understanding what meaningful work actually is
- ability to define or measure it
- understanding of the different ways in which it can be found.

---

11   www.abs.gov.au/articles/cultural-diversity-australia

THREE KEY MESSAGES

Let's go back to our definition of meaningful work:

> Meaningful work is the importance an individual places on their work meeting their current personal beliefs, values, goals, expectations, and purpose in the context of their social and cultural environment.

There are three key messages you can take from this if you want to seek meaningful work yourself, or if you are trying to provide more meaningful work for your team. The first we have touched on already.

1. Everyone's path to meaningful work is unique

Sit with that for a moment. It's crucial that it sinks in. We're not always good, us humans, at realising others don't see the world the way we do. The way work is meaningful to me may not be the way it is meaningful to you. And that is okay.

2. There are four factors of meaningful work

There are four factors to meaningful work:

- individual
- job
- organisation
- societal.

And there are many different subsets within those four factors. Which of those factors is more influential to one person may not be so much to another. There is no right or wrong. This is why finding meaningful work and providing it is somewhat of a Holy Grail.

The great news, though, is there are some factors that are more popular than others. I love asking people what they think the top three factors of meaningful work are – and the answers are often as varied as the people giving them. That's why I asked you to jot them down in the first chapter. You might have hit on one or two of the top three. In 2019 the third most popular factor of meaningful work for Australians was work that makes a difference. The second was culture, and the most popular factor, the one that people often don't guess, was having the trust of your managers. If you've ever heard the saying 'people join an organisation but leave a leader', that is this factor in a nutshell.

If you or the leaders in your organisation can work with your team-mates to build trusting relationships, this will go a long way to providing your team with meaningful work. What makes this challenging however is that also high up the list of popular factors was having clear direction from your manager. You might be thinking, *well of course, who doesn't want to know what their manager expects of them?* But the tension between providing clear direction and trusting your team is where leadership often falls down. Too much direction and people feel like they are being micro-managed. Too much trust and your team aren't sure what's expected of them. Clarity is kind. It's a tough balance to get right.

3. The factors of meaningful work can change over time

The third key message, the other gap we hit in the research, was that meaningful work changes over time, and it's important to check in with yourself to see if your factors of meaningful work have changed.

* * *

As we get into the detail and the personal stories, remember these three simple key messages. As you do the exercises in the book, or as you take the Meaningful Work Profile Tool online,[12] those three messages will help shape your thinking to allow you to understand the ways in which work can become more meaningful for you.

---

12 www.meaningfulwork.com.au

CHAPTER 3
MEANINGFUL WORK PERSONAL QUEST: *Todd Halliday*

Todd Halliday is the Principal and Managing Partner of Northrop Consulting Engineers, where he has worked for over 18 years. Northrop is a locally owned engineering consultancy with 10 offices and over 550 employees across New South Wales, Victoria, Queensland and the Australian Capital Territory. Todd has also been a Director of Northrop and served on the Board and as President of the Association of Consulting Structural Engineers, NSW. Todd, as you will see, has had quite a traditional and stable career path. Todd always knew what he wanted to do; his path to being an engineer was always clear to him. But it took five jobs in his first eight years of employment to work out what kind of organisation was right for him. Todd's story is a great example of someone who has consistently and persistently applied the theory, sometimes without knowing it, and who now consciously practises the lessons of meaningful work.

As a child, Todd didn't really think about meaning as such; he just did what he enjoyed doing, and he enjoyed drawing things, building things and designing things. People around him kept telling him he'd be a great engineer; it was a natural fit for him. The choice of engineering as a career matched his individual factors of meaningful work from an early age. Not for Todd any of the wondering what meaningful work would turn out to be.

UPBRINGING AND CAREER CHOICE

There were two other aspects of his childhood that have influenced his career journey.

His dad ran a small insurance brokerage business, which his mum was also involved with. At certain points, Todd was also intimately involved in this. For example, he wrote their payroll system because he used to watch his mum writing out cheques at night and wanted to make it easier for her. He learnt a lot from watching his parents run that business, about making money, transactions and people issues. He feels that a lot of the values he learnt early on with his parents' business helped him through his career, something that engineers don't often learn at an early stage.

The second thing that helped influence his career was his involvement with the Scouts. Todd says he wasn't a particularly social child, or particularly good at sports, so he got into Scouts and made really good friends there; he's still friends with people from the Scout group today. He was involved from the age of eight right through to his early 20s. With parents he describes as loving but hands off, with the Scouts he would often go on expeditions into the Blue Mountains for a week or so where he would have no parental oversight. He loved it. It taught him so many skills that set him up for success in his career. He had to plan for all his food, prepare routes and maps, let the scout leaders, local police and the parents know where they were going, then head off. He talks of the strategic thinking, and the balance of adventure and prudence required for those trips, as being crucial in giving him confidence and resilience that was instilled in him from a young age.

He also talks about the teamwork involved, that his personal sense of risk-taking and adventure only comes with a team around him. He still carries these values with him today.

POOR CULTURE FITS

Todd studied engineering at University of Technology, Sydney. While studying he was also working in the engineering department at the Roads & Traffic Authority (RTA) of NSW (now Transport NSW). This was a role that for the most part he did not find meaningful. His work included planning for the placement of street signs. He found that the culture was very unproductive at the time, and despite being in the engineering department, his role was more process driven. He couldn't articulate it, but it was the lack of a clear outcome and a poor culture that he struggled with. However, he does remember with some fondness some of the work; one such memory was of a right-hand turn bay on a road he designed somewhere that is still in existence.

From there, Todd went to a builder-developer where he worked for 18 months. Certain aspects of this job he thoroughly enjoyed. He'd be given a design and he'd have to organise the project, and he would find it very satisfying being part of seeing it through to completion. Having come from somewhere without clear outcomes, that combination of seeing his drive for problem-solving, ingenuity and collaboration come together was much more satisfying to Todd. His individual and job factors of meaningful work were being met. However, on an organisational level, it wasn't the right company for him. It was a six-day week role with long hours, and bearing in mind this was 30 years ago, the culture didn't sit comfortably with Todd. It was very unhealthy. Todd tells that they would knock off at 1 pm on Saturdays and go drinking. Most people smoked. It was, in Todd's words, 'very construction-blokey, and everything that comes with that'. What was interesting for Todd in this role and in the RTA was that it was the things that interfered with getting the job done that took away meaning for him. The job itself was never the issue – but it was time to look for something more meaningful.

A mentor recommended to Todd that he do some design work, and encouraged Todd to learn the science behind buildings for two to three years, saying that would be with him forever and he could go back to building later if he wanted to. Todd took this advice and joined Baigent's, a consulting engineering firm headquartered out of Melbourne, Victoria. Todd was based in Sydney and thoroughly enjoyed many of the factors of the work. He loved the intelligence, the problem-solving and the collaborative nature of working on a project with the architects and builders. You can see Todd's face light up when he's talking about a project, especially when he describes the 'second hit of meaning when it's done and you see people using it, and they don't know the engineering behind it'. Legacy is an important factor of meaningful work for Todd. He still remembers projects he did 30 years ago. He likes it when he drives past projects he designed a number of years ago and has a quiet satisfaction of thinking to himself, *I did that.*

While he was at Baigent's, he studied a master's degree. He has a strength in curiosity and has a real love of learning. This comes through as problem-solving in his engineering, and we will see it later in his people leadership too. Todd stayed with Baigent's for four years, but ultimately left because again the organisational factor wasn't quite right for him. The individual and job factors were being met (he was clear from the outset that engineering was always right for him!) but Baigent's was headquartered in Victoria and the Sydney office had shrunk considerably and wasn't getting the support Todd felt it needed. Meanwhile, the person who had given him the advice about working for a design firm had an opportunity working directly with him back in the construction side of things. Todd joined him, where he worked for nine months before heading to London.

In London, Todd found himself for the first time working for a large engineering house, Connell Mott MacDonald (now Mott MacDonald), which at the time had approximately 7000 employees in the United Kingdom. He talks of the great culture it had, being employee owned, but still feeling a bit 'like a number' being so big. He loved the work. He was involved in some great projects. He talks with deep delight about the project he was involved with for the new Farringdon Station. He also recalls how his somewhat cavalier attitude actually helped his career. This was in 2002, and Todd describes a hierarchical, formal structure. Culturally it was quite different to Australia. Todd was not a man who wore a tie to work. He was not a man who played golf, regardless of whether it was the boss who had invited him. He ended up with a bit of a reputation as this 'larrikin Australian' (his words!) who had direct access to the Directors because he didn't worry about the social etiquette, and if he had something to say, he'd just go up and talk to them. He did quite well from that point of view.

When the time came for Todd to return to Australia, he was very conscious that he'd had five jobs in eight years. He was in his early 30s, and looking at his resumé he wanted to find something he could be sure he could have on his CV for at least the next five years. He spent some time thinking about what had worked and what hadn't for him in his career to date. He knew the individual and job factors that worked for him. It was important to maintain those aspects of problem-solving, curiosity and collaboration. He had learnt that the organisational factor, for him, needed to include having the owners of the business close by and within the business. This had come from his experiences with the RTA and Baigent's. He also knew he wanted something where he could make improvements, where he could use his curiosity beyond the limits of his job description. At Baigent's he'd written a programme on Microsoft Access to make their timesheets electronic, because they were processing them manually, just as he had helped his mum and dad with their payroll system all those years before. These aspects of continual improvement were important to him.

EVERYTHING COMES TOGETHER

In his next role at Northrop all these things came together. There was, naturally, the engineering side, and he could build up his own base of clients. It was a partnership-based organisation with the opportunity for performance-based equity. Todd could see there were plenty of business improvements he could get involved with too.

Todd has been with Northrop for 18 years. He has been Principal, Structural Engineer, then Principal, Sydney Regional Manager and now Principal, Managing Partner. There have been plenty of times when he has had his share of frustrations. But this time, unlike in his other roles, it has been the organisational factor that has kept him there and seen him through. He loves the culture at Northrop, and has built great relationships there over the years. He is a big believer in the organisation.

The significant change in meaningful work within Northrop for Todd came when he started managing people. Not as part of a project team, which he'd been doing from an engineering perspective for a while, but as a people leader on an ongoing basis. This came in his mid-30s. He says he made every mistake possible. He was impatient. He had high expectations, assuming people would just magically do what he wanted. He didn't spend any time helping them understand why they should do what he was asking. He didn't set timeframes. And eventually he'd just get in there and do it himself out of frustration.

I suspect he may not have been as bad as he makes out, but if so, he would be a great example of the fact that people can learn leadership. He was so bad, he says, that he quite seriously thought about going back to being a structural engineer within the firm but was talked out of it. Instead, he went on a leadership training programme. And then, as the engineer Todd is, a funny thing happened. He became fascinated by the science of human behaviour. In fact, he became somewhat hooked on it. He started learning everything he could and applying an engineering approach to leading people. He feels he took a too blunt approach at first – you could say he ... overengineered it (sorry, couldn't help myself!). But as he learned more and practised more, leadership became more natural and nuanced for him.

Todd also correlates his improvement in people leadership and his love of it with the timing of having children. This is a great example of how a societal factor of meaningful work can impact on our psychological perspective. No longer being on the tools, as the Sydney Regional Manager of Northrop by this point, Todd says being a parent gave him a greater level of care, empathy and nurturing. It also allowed him to understand that sometimes people, no matter their age, need to hear things two, three, maybe four times to truly understand, and it helps if they know why they are doing something. He also mentioned that it gave him a much better understanding of other parents and families. Further, it anchored him individually and made him think more about his own health and wellbeing.

Todd became a Managing Partner in April 2022, which was somewhat accidental. I say this because Todd is not ambitious in the traditional sense of the word. He often thinks to himself, *how has this career happened?* But the kick he gets out of engineering the design to build a school he knows others will use for years to come is the same kick he gets out of his leadership journey. For him, leadership is about servitude. It's about helping the others in the team be successful.

We've touched before on the balance Todd has between adventure and prudence, and his desire to be part of a collaborative team. Northrop is a partnership, performance-based organisation. A few years ago, Todd and other members of the partnership were discussing the strategy and future of the organisation. Todd, having already decided it was time for him to move on, offered up some somewhat frank advice for where he thought Northrop should head strategically. The kind of advice you may not offer if you were planning on staying. Turns out the rest of the Board of Northrop agreed, and they convinced Todd to stay on as a Managing Partner instead of moving on as planned.

Todd has been interested in the science of human behaviour since his first leadership course nearly 15 years ago. I first introduced him to the theory of meaningful work two years ago. Northrop have done a lot of work internally on some elements around creating meaningful workplaces. They have done some excellent strategy work around their culture, on growth mindset for example. They've always worked with a 'client-side thinking' approach which had them focusing on the people at the hearts of their projects. They are now talking about 'meaningful opportunities' from an internal perspective, thinking about how their people feel about their jobs day to day. They are a people-led organisation, and they see how it livens up every conversation they have internally and how it differentiates them from a talent attraction, retention and development perspective. It also lights up Todd's face when he talks about it. It's great to see he's taking his love of meaningful work forward for a whole group of people within his organisation, one of the first leaders genuinely committing to creating meaningful work company-wide. I can't wait to see what the future holds for Northrop.

CHAPTER 4
THE FIRST FACTOR OF MEANINGFUL WORK: INDIVIDUAL

(This chapter contributed to by Rebecca Rynehart)

THE INDIVIDUAL FACTOR: 'IT'S ALL ABOUT YOU!'

The first factor of meaningful work is the individual factor. The subsets of this look at how our interests, our abilities, our personality, our traits, our goals and our personal narratives affect how much meaning we derive from our work.

A good way to understand these factors is to think of a job that in many ways would suit these aspects of your personality, but for one specific area. For me, being a librarian comes to mind. I have a deep love of books, and love spending time in libraries. I hold strong beliefs about the importance of the written word and the impact it can have, and feel deeply about the power education has to change lives and the role of the library as part of this. I'm also an avid reader. From an interests, abilities, goals and personal narratives perspective, being a librarian could be deeply meaningful for me. However, I'm also an extrovert. So, spending my days in an environment where I would need to be quiet and not talk too much would be a real struggle. Great role and *almost* a perfect fit on the individual level, but ultimately this wouldn't fit the mould for meaningful work for me.

Let me share the story of someone who found meaningful work through thinking about individual factors. Rebecca Rynehart is the General Manager of the Consulting business in Beaumont People. She is responsible for all the consulting and professional development services we offer in the employee lifecycle that sit outside our recruitment process. It is a business she has established and built from within our organisation. It came about as a result of her understanding what meaningful work was to her.

Rebecca joined us in 2020. Prior to this she was running her own consulting business. This had been a lifelong dream of hers, something she wanted to do so she could create more meaning in work for others and contribute to a higher purpose, while having the freedom to design her work how she wanted to. But having been on this journey, what Rebecca realised was she was missing the connection and culture that comes from working within a team. On the individual level, teamwork is part of Rebecca's personal narrative, and her personality is such that she finds working as part of a team, collaborating and building on ideas together, suits her individually much more than working alone.

Further, Rebecca had done a little homework on us as an organisation, and when a maternity leave position became available, she applied. Interestingly, she wasn't necessarily the best suited on paper for the position. In fact, I initially told our internal talent manager that I didn't want to pursue her application. But Rebecca did something fantastic. She used her individual skills and personality traits to put together a video as to why she would be great for the role. Her initiative was so impressive we gave her the contract, and after successfully completing it, we kept her on part time and she endeavoured to build the consulting business from within Beaumont People. She has done this very successfully. She still has a lot of the freedom she was looking for that running her own business also afforded, but with the support and framework of a team around her. She has always continued working with us part time to allow her the freedom to continue her personal enterprise, while allowing her to build something with us that gives her the people connection and contribution that is so meaningful to her.

As an exercise now, take a minute to think about the individual factors of meaningful work. Jot down some answers to the comments below as to what makes work meaningful for you on an individual level. If you find this hard, think about a time when you have been enthusiastic at work, and a time when you have been frustrated, to see if it helps you to think about the answers.

The interests I have and enjoy using in a work environment are:
Think here about the things you enjoy doing, the practical day to-day-stuff that interests you. Is it interacting with customers? Doing something creative? Being physical in work? Understanding a complex theory? Spending time on the details? What else?

_____

_____

_____

_____

My abilities (the things I'm good at) in a work context are:
These are the things you are genuinely good at, the aspects of work where other people say to you, 'You're brilliant at that, how do you do it?' and you may think, 'I have no idea, I just do it'. Because often when we are good at something it doesn't feel hard. It's also the things

you do where time flies, you are in a 'flow' state, and you become energised by undertaking that activity.

_____

_____

_____

I know that when I get to use the following aspects of my personality, I really enjoy work:

This one is about your character traits – are you quiet or loud? Are you a thinker or a doer? Do you like fast paced, or prefer the time to look for detail and accuracy? Are you interested in people or things? Are you funny? Considered? Thoughtful? Kind? Determined? Calm? Have a think about the personality traits you love about yourself, and list them here.

_____

_____

_____

My personal goals in work in the next three years are:

This one is about YOUR personal goals, not your boss's, not your team's, not your organisation's. Not what you see on social media, or what your friends or family think you should be doing. Is it that you want a promotion; if so, why? Is it that you want to do enough to have security and enjoy your life outside of work? What are you trying to achieve? Are you thinking about completely changing careers, and if so, why?

_____

_____

_____

The story I tell myself about the importance of my work is:

This is an important question to think about to understand the role work plays in your life. Is work a big piece of your self-identity? Is what you do integral to who you are? Or is it in line with other aspects of your life? Or, in fact is it not important at all, merely a way to pay the bills and allow you to pursue other interests? What are your personal values, and do they align with the work you do?

THE INDIVIDUAL FACTOR IS ALIGNED TO A STRENGTHS-BASED APPROACH

One of the most tried-and-tested ways organisations help people to understand the individual factors of meaningful work is using strengths profiling. There is significant evidence that understanding and working to your strengths can result in less stress, higher engagement, higher vitality, higher self-esteem and higher performance, and you are more likely to reach your goals.

Our strengths can come from nature, nurture or experience, and they can shift and change over the course of our lives. In addition to the work benefits listed above we are also happier[13], and can be more resilient when we use our strengths more.[14] Simply knowing our strengths and weaker areas is a primary step towards developing self-awareness. Increased self-awareness has many benefits, including self-acceptance[15] and confidence while at work. Research has shown

---

13   Govindji R. & Linley P. A. (2007). 'Strength's use, self-concordance and wellbeing: implications for strengths coaching and coaching psychologists'. *Int. Coach. Psychol. Rev.*
14   CAPP (2010). 'Technical manual and statistical properties for Realise2'. Coventry, UK: CAPP.
15   www.psychcentral.com/health/self-awareness#benefits.

self-awareness training can improve communication with colleagues and job-related wellbeing.[16] Clearly self-awareness is an important muscle for us to develop in life; however, according to Tasha Eurich, an expert on the subject, *95 per cent of us think we are self-aware but only about 10 to 15 per cent of us actually are.* That's a pretty scary gap![17]

Evidence-based research for using strengths more

Less stress[18]

Reach goals[22]

Employee engagement[19]

Self-awareness

Performance[21]

Vitality, self-esteem[20]

16 Sutton, A., Williams, H.M. & Allinson, C.W. (2015), 'A longitudinal, mixed method evaluation of self-awareness training in the workplace', *European Journal of Training and Development*, Vol. 39 No. 7, pp. 610-627.

17 'Working with people who aren't self aware', Tasha Eurich, October 2018, Difficult Conversations, *Harvard Business Review.*

18 Wood, A. M., Linley, P. A., Maltby, J., Kashdan, T. B. & Hurling, R. (2011). 'Using personal and psychological strengths leads to increases in well-being over time: A longitudinal study and the development of the strengths use questionnaire'. *Personality and Individual Differences*, 50(1), 15-19.

19 Minhas, G. (2010). 'Developing realised and unrealised strengths: Implications for engagement, self-esteem, life satisfaction and well-being'. *Assessment & Development Matters*, 2(1), 12-6.
    Harter, J. K., Schmidt, F. L. & Hayes, T. L. (2002). 'Business-unit-level relationship between employee satisfaction, employee engagement, and business outcomes: A meta-analysis'. *Journal of Applied Psychology*, 87(2), 268-279.

20 Govindji, R. & Linley, P. A. (2007). 'Strengths use, self-concordance and well-being: Implications for strengths coaching and coaching psychologists'. *International Coaching Psychology Review*, 2(2), 143-153.
    Wood, A. M., Linley, P. A., Maltby, J., Kashdan, T. B. & Hurling, R. (2011). 'Using personal and psychological strengths leads to increases in well-being over time: A longitudinal study and the development of the strengths use questionnaire'. *Personality and Individual Differences*, 50(1), 15-19.

21 Corporate Leadership Council (2002). Performance management survey. Washington, DC.

22 Linley, P.A., Nielsen, K., Wood, A.M., Gillett, R. & Biswas-Diener, R. (2010). 'Using signature strengths in pursuit of goals: Effects on goal progress, need satisfaction, and well-being, and implications for coaching psychologists'. *International Coaching Psychology Review.*

A BIT OF SELF-REFLECTION

There are a number of methods you can consider to discover your own strengths and those of your people. First you can simply observe yourself or others if you are a leader, as I'm suggesting here. A bit of self-reflection. In fact, let's try it now.

What skills or traits would you describe as your strengths? Would others agree or come up with differing traits?

Don't think here about your typical interview answer. This question is for the benefit of no-one but yourself. The question is not 'what do you think your greatest strengths should be?' but rather 'what are they?' If you struggle to genuinely answer that, think about what gives you energy – what do you LOVE to do? What, when asked, triggers the little voice in your head to say 'hell, yeah!'? Your answers to this question may be quite similar to the answers in the first question on the individual aspects of meaningful work, or they may have triggered different responses, which may help you to refine that first answer.

As a leader it is also important to ask yourself these questions in relation to your team members. The more you can help your team work to their strengths the better the outcomes will be.

The second method for assessing strengths is simply to have a conversation. You can discuss with your coworkers, your manager or your direct reports. You can discuss with your family and friends. You may help each other identify strengths that you don't recognise in yourselves, and it may help you bring strengths from one environment, say your social environment, into another, say your work environment.

As an exercise, next time you have a willing group, try this. Each person has a piece of A4 paper. On the top of the page you write your top three strengths, with one line against each about how or when you use that strength. Then you fold the paper so you can still see the name but not the strengths underneath. You pass the paper to your left, and you do the same now for the person who was next to you. But this time you are writing what you think their strengths are, with a one line example of when you've seen that happen. You continue this until you receive back the paper with your own name at the top and then enjoy reading about all the ways in which you are fabulous. Aside from making you feel great, you can use this exercise in the following discussion.

Which strengths came up consistently? Are you using those strengths in all your environments, and is there a possibility you may be overplaying those strengths?

_____

_____

Which strengths that others listed about you surprised you? Why? How do you think you could make more of those strengths?

_____

_____

Which individuals within your group had contradictory strengths (where they are seemingly the opposite of each other)? Does this provide diversity of thinking or tension? How can you work better together to tip the balance towards diversity of thinking rather than tension in the team?

_____

_____

Is there anything within your group that could be shifted, reassigned or changed to allow people to work more to their strengths?

_____

_____

Finally, the most thorough assessment method is formally measuring your strengths. There are a number of tools that do this. I use the Strengths Profile.[23] One of the things I love about this is it provides feedback on four different areas of your strengths:

- your realised strengths
- your unrealised strengths
- your learned behaviours
- your weaknesses.

There is real value in knowing more about your unrealised strengths because these are the ones you are not using as much as you could in the workplace. This gives you an opportunity to think about how you could bring more strengths into your day to day. It also helps you in understanding which strengths you could be overplaying, and how to ensure you get the balance right.

In 2020, when I first took a Strengths Profile, 'curiosity' and 'writing' came up as two of my unrealised strengths. This gave me the opportunity to think about how I could incorporate them more into my work. As a result, I worked on a number of leadership presentations which we turned into webinars for our community, at a time when they needed connection most. I would research the topics our

---

23   Strengths Profile is a product by Cappfinity.

clients and candidates had said would be of interest and then write the content for the presentations, and where needed, help source a speaker. Our first ever webinar was on 1 April 2020, and during the pandemic we provided content and speakers for numerous webinars that reached an audience of hundreds, quite possibly thousands, across Australia and also, I believe, into the US, the UK, Europe and NZ. I remember being surprised by the quantity of people who would turn up and the range of regions they'd come from. People told us at the time that it was often the highlight of their week. Business was slow as a result of the pandemic, which enabled me to use those two unrealised strengths while also helping others by providing content that was useful in challenging circumstances. Further, knowing that 'writer' was one of my unrealised strengths has been a catalyst for me writing this book!

ASSESSING THE TEAM

There is great power as a leader in helping your team understand their strengths and working together on them. Using the formal Strengths Profile also allows me to generate a separate team strengths report which can show you where your team strengths come together and in which specific strengths you may not have as much capacity. As you attract new people to your team, you can assess which areas of strengths you need to build more capacity in to optimise your team performance.

Understanding each other's strengths in a team gives you a language with which to understand different approaches. A common example we use is that of the 'action' versus 'incubator' strengths. People with action as a strength like to make quick decisions and move on things, and prefer momentum to anything else. Incubators like to ponder over ideas, think through the pros and cons, and ensure they've had enough time to truly assess a problem. People with these somewhat contradictory strengths can find themselves in conflict. But we all recognise we need both capabilities in the workplace.

As an action person, if I know someone is an incubator, I'm more likely to say, 'How much time do you need to think this through?' or, 'This is a situation that calls for deep thought and consideration, let's get our incubator onto it.' Or, when I'm frustrated, 'Seriously, can we just get on with it?' (Let's be real here!)

Knowing each team member's strengths allows the leader to allocate resources to a project accordingly, to foster partnerships and collaborations, to uncover hidden value and, ultimately, this allows the leader to move towards a more outcome-based, mission-aligned way of delivering.

WORKING TOGETHER

The real power of working to your strengths is when you become aware of working with other people and knowing their strengths. If I use Rebecca Rynehart again as an example, how we work together has really shown us the power of this. When you know each other's strengths, unrealised strengths and weaknesses you can help bring out the best in each other, which really helps to generate meaningful work aligned to your individual factor.

Using the action strength provides a good example. It is one of my top strengths; I'm incredibly action oriented. In fact, I am often at risk of overplaying it. Back in the day, it made me a very good temp recruiter because then quick action and quick thinking was essential. But as a managing director, time to think and reflect is important. Rebecca, as a trusted colleague, knows this about me. She also knows that curiosity is a strength of mine. She is very good at spotting when I might be moving too quickly and asking intelligent, thought-provoking questions that spark my curiosity. This gets me thinking and makes me investigate things more deeply before I take action. She uses one of my strengths to counteract a different one, which helps me change tack when I need to.

I do the same with her. One of her biggest strengths is mission. It is important to her that she understands how her work aligns to her vocation. However, one of her weaknesses is persistence. Knowing this about Rebecca, on occasion, if she has struggled with some momentum behind a project, I have worked with her to reframe what she is doing. We'll talk through how we can take it back to the mission to get some new energy behind it, and that helps Rebecca to be reinvigorated.

Finally, we have helped each other where we have matching strengths. We both have curiosity as a strength which means we spark off each other. We often co-create content, build on each other's ideas or explore further a topic one of us has initiated.

* * *

When we work to our strengths, we are more motivated, we are aligned with our individual traits and also more likely to be working in line with our personal narrative and therefore strongly meeting the needs of meaningful work on the individual level. Understanding our individual factor is the first step in bringing the four factors of meaningful work together. Let's now turn to the second factor of meaningful work.

CHAPTER 5

THE SECOND FACTOR OF MEANINGFUL WORK: JOB

IS IT REALLY AS SIMPLE AS 'FIND A JOB YOU'LL LOVE AND YOU'LL NEVER HAVE TO WORK A DAY IN YOUR LIFE'?

The second factor of meaningful work is the job factor. This is about how much the job has been designed to enable meaningful work. It looks at the type of work, the quality of work and the amount of work involved in the job, as well as how much the organisation allows the job to be modified to cater for someone's meaningful work needs.

A good way to think about this is, first, around your job expectations. For example, how important are your work conditions to you? How much control do you need over your job? And how important is it to you that you have opportunities to develop your career?

Beyond your expectations of the job itself, it's about how much meaning you derive from your work when it is valued by others; when you understand how it contributes to the organisation's objectives; and how much opportunity you have to influence the way you do your job.

When I think about the job factor, I often think about accountants. This is because I spent five years of my life recruiting accountants and, in that time, I estimate I interviewed nearly 2000 accountants, placing one or two people a week, on average, into an accounting role. I learnt a thing or two about their jobs. One of the key things that struck me was how most position descriptions for financial accountants were very similar across different companies, and even industries. You often couldn't tell the difference, in any significant way, between the roles, based on the position description alone. On paper, the roles looked very similar.

But what became apparent to me, as a recruiter, was that this couldn't be further from the truth. The volume of work, the deadlines, the systems all varied dramatically. The support and training these people received was quite different between different organisations. The variety and complexity in the roles was astoundingly diverse. These variables meant that how meaningful a candidate would find their potential new role really needed to be investigated to ensure a good match.

Often, as recruiters, we experience people who don't understand that it is not the job factor that is undermining their ability to find meaningful work. People come to us and say, for example, 'I'm not sure what I'm really looking for, all I do know is that I no longer wish to be an accountant' (in this example). I have personally fallen into this trap. Earlier in my career, I spent some time and energy investigating how I could get out of recruitment as a profession. I had decided it wasn't for me, I wasn't enjoying my work in the way I wanted to. I networked with a number of people in aligned professional services to try to assess what kind of sideways move I might make to change careers. Then through a happy accident, I changed roles within the same industry. I discovered that I did, indeed, still love our profession. People are my jam! It was rather that I wasn't aligned to the organisational factor of meaningful work in my previous company (which we'll come to shortly). I didn't realise this was the issue, however, because there was absolutely nothing wrong with my previous organisation, in fact it was great in many ways. If you remember our first key message: everyone's path to meaningful work is unique. It was simply not the right organisation for me.

So, let's take a moment of self-reflection to think about how the job factor impacts your meaningful work. Think about the questions below and jot down some answers.

How important are your work conditions to you?

Think about whether you speak up when you or others are treated unfairly, and, if so, why?

Think about whether career development is critical to you or whether you're happy as is.

Think about your work environment, the tools of your trade, the volume and complexity of your work. How important are these things to you, and if they are important what could you tweak to move the dial to make your role more meaningful?

Jot down your thoughts below.

_____

_____

_____

How much are you able to design or modify your job to enable more meaning?

Think about whether you need clarity on how your role contributes to the bigger picture and whether you have that clarity.

Think about whether you are intrinsically motivated or whether you need to know your work is valued by others. This is about how much freedom you have over your day, your workload and your ability to control the duties within your role.

Jot down your thoughts below.

_____

_____

_____

TWEAKING THE JOB FACTOR

We have a fabulous example in-house of how we have been able to adapt two roles within our organisation to allow more meaning in work. In 2021 we took on two part-time marketing coordinators to support our Head of Marketing. Both roles saw two near-graduates join us as they finished their degrees. Initially we split the roles around functions. We have two major cohorts we market to, clients and candidates, so one person took each cohort and did all the marketing activities associated with that contingent. As the team graduated, and we continued to grow, we were able to take them both on full time.

We used that period to review how well we had set up this blossoming team. In discussion with them, Sarah, our Head of Marketing, realised they both loved some parts of their jobs, but both had aspects of their roles that simply didn't float their boats. Sarah was able to review their strength profiles and meaningful work profiles to understand what could work instead. As a result, the team completely re-jigged who was responsible for what, which allowed both team members to spend their days doing the things that lit them up. Talk about a win–win–win. Win for them, win for us, and win for our external community. This is the power of tweaking the job factor of meaningful work.

CHAPTER 6
THE THIRD FACTOR OF MEANINGFUL WORK: ORGANISATION

DON'T WE ALL KNOW THAT CULTURE EATS STRATEGY FOR BREAKFAST?

The third factor of meaningful work is the organisational factor. This is another common 'go-to' factor for people when seeking meaningful work. It relates to all the aspects of work that make it meaningful from the organisational level. The subsets of this factor are leadership, organisational culture, organisational policies and practices, and the social environment at work.

A common question we are asked when sharing our research about meaningful work is how our Meaningful Work Profile Tool (MWPT – of which more later) is different to other engagement or culture surveys. This question itself shows how easily we are confused by what meaningful work actually is, and is telling in why we struggle so much to define it, find it or provide it. Engagement and culture surveys are highly valuable tools which measure specific aspects within an organisation.

Typically, though, they only take in the individual's view of the organisation. Culture surveys take a measure of culture – which is only one subset of one of the four factors of meaningful work. Engagement tools seek to understand how engaged your people are, whereas research shows that people in meaningful work are more engaged, so thinking about and understanding meaningful work is a lead indicator, which will result in higher engagement levels from the outset.[24]

Remember our definition of meaningful work:

> Meaningful work is the importance an individual places on their work meeting their current personal beliefs, values, goals, expectations, and purpose in the context of their social and cultural environment.

When reminded of this definition it becomes easier to put the organisational factor into context as one of the four factors of meaningful work.

Often, when we look at the organisational factor of meaningful work, we can see how the various aspects we have been discussing come together. Remembering that everyone's path to meaningful work is unique demonstrates how looking at engagement or culture surveys can help move a company towards the most 'popular view', which isn't necessarily the best way to optimise meaningful work for that organisation.

For example, because there is significant evidence[25] that those who have a strong social environment at work and who build friendships at work are more engaged and more productive, most engagement or

24 Awang, Z., Ahmed, U., Hoque, A. S. M. M., Siddiqui, B. A., Dahri, A. S. & Muda, H. (2017). 'The mediating role of meaningful work in the relationship between career growth opportunities and work engagement'.
25 www.gallup.com/workplace/397058/increasing-importance-best-friend-work.aspx
www.hrnews.co.uk/work-friends-makes-us-more-productive-according-to-research/
www.europeansting.com/2019/11/25/why-its-good-to-turn-your-colleagues-into-friends/

culture surveys assume that if I don't have friends at work, I am disengaged and unproductive. This may be true for a majority of people, but it is misleading to try to lump all employees into that category. If you are someone for whom making friends at work isn't important (perhaps you are an introvert, or perhaps you are at a stage in life where your out-of-work commitments mean you struggle to maintain more friendships), making an assumption that just because you don't have friends at work makes you a disengaged employee may well be false.

HOW DOES THE ORGANISATIONAL FACTOR OF MEANINGFUL WORK SHOW UP?

So, how does the organisational factor of meaningful work show up in the real world, and how do you know if this is the area you need to think about for yourself in seeking meaningful work? If you are a leader, how do you know if you are providing the organisational factor of meaningful work?

You've likely come across the phrase, 'people don't leave organisations, they leave leaders'. Well, it's true. Leadership is one of the most commonly quoted aspects of meaningful work. In our 2019 survey results, having the trust of your manager was the most popular factor of meaningful work. And the importance of leadership on meaningful work didn't change through Covid, but there was a shift in what people wanted from their leaders. Conscious and compassionate leadership became key, with survey results from the 2021–22 data showing 86 per cent of people needed the organisation they work for to care about their wellbeing.

If you are still wondering to yourself how you separate the organisational factor from the other factors of meaningful work, let's revisit my earlier example of my alternative life as a librarian. In the individual factor chapter, I referenced the fact that this type of work wouldn't work for me because I'm an extrovert. Let's assume then, in this case, I'm not. So, working as a librarian could be the perfect role for me. I love books, I have strong personal value about education and the importance of reading, and I enjoy a quiet work environment. The role of librarian is looking more and more appealing. But let's say the other librarians at my workplace are particularly cliquey, and my boss is uncaring and does not provide clear direction, and the procedures I have to follow are overly complex and don't help our customer base. As a result, all the meaning I may have otherwise found in my role has been undone by these poor organisational factors.

Let's now take some time for you to think about how the organisational factors affect your personal quest for meaningful work.

Jot down some answers to the areas below as to what makes work meaningful for you on an organisational level. If you find this hard, think about a time when you have been enthusiastic about your work in areas that are unrelated specifically to your job, and conversely, a time when you have been frustrated at an organisational level; that is, whether you were the CEO or the receptionist your enthusiasm and frustrations about the organisation would be the same.

When has the leadership of an organisation inspired you?

Think beyond one specific person to the leadership more generally. Was there a consistent culture among your leaders? What was it about the leadership culture that made it great? Has a great leadership culture motivated you? When have you worked for poor leaders? Did this affect your motivation levels? What type of leadership gets the best out of you?

_____

_____

How important is it for you to know what the organisational goals are and how you are contributing towards those goals?

Can you think of a time when you have had real clarity on where the company is going, and the difference your work made? If so, how did this make you feel? If not, is it because it's not important to you? Or have you sometimes thought to yourself 'I don't really understand the difference my work makes', and did that thought demotivate you?

_____

_____

What type of culture gets the best out of you?

Do you need a workplace that is innovative and creative? Could you or have you worked for an organisation that provides products and services that conflict with your ethics and values?

_____

_____

How important are working relationships to you?

How social do you need your workplace to be? How collaborative? Do you like the opportunity to make new friends at work? Is it important to you that you are supported by the people you work with?

_____

_____

What do the practices of your organisation mean to you?

Is it important to you that the organisation you work for gives back to the community and makes a meaningful difference to people's lives? If so, in what ways? Do those ways align with the kinds of organisations you have worked with? How important is it for you that the organisation makes a profit and you make a good salary compared with contributing to society?

_____

_____

Sometimes we think we are unhappy at work because we've chosen the wrong profession, but before you spend time and money retraining yourself, it's worth assessing if a different type of organisation in the same profession might just make the difference you need for your work to become meaningful.

CHAPTER 7

THE FOURTH FACTOR OF MEANINGFUL WORK: SOCIETAL

ULTIMATELY, WE DO ALL CARE WHAT OUR FRIENDS AND FAMILY THINK!

Sometimes though, one of the biggest factors of meaningful work is the one over which we have the least control. The fourth and final factor of meaningful work is the societal factor.

This is the factor those of us raised and living in Western societies often overlook. We touched on this factor when we discussed why our research was a world first and what the integrated approach of both the psychological and the sociological factors mean. Let's spend a little more time now on the societal factor so you can really start to understand how it may have influenced you in your search for meaningful work.

When we first looked into the research this was where we realised there was a gap. A truly sociological approach hadn't been fully adopted in any of the tools that measured meaningful work, but the social value of work was an important consideration when defining and evaluating meaningful work. This is why we took an integrated approach that looked at both the psychological and sociological factors. We recognised that meaningful works sits within a complex relationship between the individual, job, organisation, as well as within the society and culture the individual finds themselves in. Meaningful work needs to be viewed holistically to truly understand it, and getting to the heart of the societal factor is the key to unlocking the final piece of it.

The societal factor takes into consideration how much value society assigns to the work we do. It also considers the economic and social influences that affect how someone attains meaning in their job. Access to decent work and cultural norms are key.

Let's break those things down.

HOW MUCH VALUE SOCIETY ASSIGNS TO THE WORK WE DO

First let's look at how much value society assigns to the work we do.

I came across a great example of how this specific aspect of the societal factor of meaningful work can impact us day to day in Annabel Crabb's well-articulated book *The Wife Drought: Why Women Need Wives and Men Need Lives*. This example goes beyond even the work itself, to specific skills within the workplace. In this book Crabb discusses the gender pay gap and the often-quoted reason for it. The narrative goes that the reason for the gender pay gap is because men can negotiate better than women, and if women got better at negotiating salary, then the gender pay gap would improve. Crabb goes on to evidence how, in actuality, both men and women are more than capable of negotiating well, but men are better at negotiating salary and women are better at negotiating flexibility. Further, she illustrates that this is not because this is what each respective gender desires, but in fact it is because that is what society tells us that it is acceptable to negotiate, according to our gender. Society assigns value to men negotiating salary and women negotiating flexibility but not the other way around. If salary is an important individual factor of meaningful work for you, but you are influenced by the societal expectation on negotiating this, there will be a conflict in how meaningful you are likely to find your work. As Annabel Crabb writes:

> The truth is that people find it easier to ask for things that they are expected to ask for. We expect women will ask for flexible work hours, or to come back to work part-time after having a baby. We expect that, because most of the time, that's what happens. We don't expect men to ask. And sure enough, they don't. Sandberg's point is that women aren't encouraged to stay in the race. But the problem for men is that no-one teaches them how to stop.[26]

We had an example of this with a person who worked with us for a short time at Beaumont People. She was doing really well, and we loved having her on the team. She was enjoying the work on all three of the psychological levels: the individual, job and organisation were all great for her. However, she came from a culture that hugely valued a university qualification, and was getting significant messaging from those close to her that this was a path she needed to take. Ultimately, she decided that the societal factor of meaningful work – that is, meeting the expectations of her family – was more important to her than the other three and left us to pursue a degree, even though she recognised this was in conflict with her psychological perspective. Understanding this helped both us and her work through the decision, and she left us with our full support. She is putting herself in a position where in the future she can find meaningful work that aligns her psychological factors with her societal ones.

---

26   *The Wife Drought*, p.70.

ACCESS TO DECENT WORK

The second part of the societal factor is access to decent work. This includes the obvious ability to access the work itself (you can't be an astronaut if you don't have access to the space station!) but it also considers how safe your working conditions are, your access to healthcare, and how well the organisational values match your personal cultural and family values. In the theory we also consider here adequate compensation and hours that allow for free time and rest.[27]

If we revisit my unlikely, alternative life as a librarian we can show how the societal factor might play out in real life. Even if I am well suited to the role, due to my personal beliefs and my interest in and ability to do the job, and if, in fact, there was a library with a great culture, leaders and practices that suited me, it would all become quickly irrelevant if I didn't live in an area with commutable access to that library. It would also be a career I would be unlikely to pursue if I didn't have access to the education and training I needed to become a librarian, or I lived in a culture that didn't value books, reading and furthering of knowledge, or I couldn't live off the librarian's salary provided.

HOW CULTURAL NORMS SHAPE THE WAY WE THINK ABOUT WORK

The final piece to consider when thinking about the societal factor is to think about how cultural norms might shape the way we think about meaningful work. Often, they play a bigger part than we realise. It's not uncommon in diverse organisations that we may have conflicting cultural norms within the same company. This subset will consider how much the organisation puts an emphasis on the individual's

---

27   This was deleted in the tool as it didn't meet the validity criteria, per later chapters.

general fulfilment and wellbeing, as well as how much the organisation puts an emphasis on work specifically as a pathway to individual fulfilment and wellbeing. Depending on the culture you were raised in, your views on those two things above might be quite different from your organisation's.

Where you sit on those cultural norms may align with a 2018 report released by PwC, 'Workforce of the future – The competing forces shaping 2030'. This report sees the world of work separating into four 'worlds', grading the axis of business fragmentation through to corporate integration on one axis and collectivism through to individualism on the other. They predict this will create four quite different worlds of work.

The Four Worlds of Work in 2030

Fragmentation

The Yellow World
Humans come first

Social-first and community businesses prosper. Crowdfunded capital flows towards ethical and blameless brands. There is a search for meaning and relevance with a social heart. Artisans, makers and 'new Worker Guilds' thrive. Humanness is highly valued.

The Red World
Innovation rules

Organisations and individuals race to give consumers what they want. Innovation outpaces regulation. Digital platforms give outsized reach and influence to those with a winning idea. Specialists and niche profit-makers flourish.

Collectivism ⟵——————————————————⟶ Individualism

The Green World
Companies care

Social responsibility and trust dominate the corporate agenda with concerns about demographic changes, climate and sustainability becoming key drivers of business.

The Blue World
Corporate is King

Big company capitalism rules as organisations continue to grow bigger and individual preferences trump beliefs about social responsibility.

Integration

I believe which of these worlds appeals to you will be highly dependent on how your cultural norms have influenced how much value you assign to these areas. Individualism and collectivism has been highly researched in cultural studies, and applying this to the work context is highly relevant.[28] Even if the worlds don't fragment quite in the way PwC predict, thinking through these defined areas in line with thinking about your own societal factors and cultural norms may help you to clarify what makes work meaningful for you, on a societal level. Remember *everyone's path to meaningful work is unique*. There is no right or wrong. This is especially true when it comes to the societal factor. It's the society you have been raised in, your culture, your beliefs, your friends and family that influence the way you think about meaningful work.

When thinking about the societal factor for yourself, taking into account the above information, it's good to consider the questions below. Again, take some time to think about these and jot down your answers, using the questions in italics to help prompt your thinking:

Has there ever been a time when you did a job because the people around you, your family, and friends, thought it would be a great job to have, even if you didn't love it?

Have you found yourself in a job you disliked but not wanting to leave for fear of disappointing someone? Have you felt pressure to continue with a role even though you knew it wasn't for you?

_____

_____

28 'The expanded view of individualism and collectivism: One, two or four dimension?', Kamal Fatehi, Jennifer L Priestley, Gita Taasoobshirazi, 7 April 2020, *International Journal of Cross Cultural Management.*

Have you ever not applied for, or turned down a job because of a concern about how those around you might react?

Perhaps you have shied away from something because people important to you have said it's not stable enough or there is not enough career opportunity. Perhaps those around you have a negative view of a profession that you would like to try – for example your family think of lawyers as 'ambulance chasers' or those around you consider academic work not hands on enough?

_____

_____

Did you ever consider a career that you didn't pursue because you didn't have the means or access to at the time?

Do you sometimes wish you had studied better at school or picked a different course at TAFE or university? Do you sometimes wish you lived closer to access to other types of career? Have your work choices been affected because you simply couldn't afford to do something you would really like to have done?

_____

_____

Have you ever felt like your organisation hasn't put enough emphasis on your individual fulfilment and wellbeing?

Did you feel like you should have been listened to more? Were you concerned that your organisation wasn't doing more to provide you with support and care? Or do you not think this is your organisation's responsibility anyway, and this sits with your own personal responsibility?

_____

_____

Have you ever considered leaving or left an organisation because they weren't proactive enough in managing your career pathway for you?

Do you expect that they should take the lead in your career progression? Would you only apply for a promotion internally if asked to do so? Or do you feel it is your, and only your, responsibility to manage your career?

_____

_____

There is absolutely nothing wrong with acknowledging how important the societal impact is. It's also worth acknowledging how it can change over time. The influence of our parents wanes as we become more independent from them. We can move and find ourselves in different cultures and with different access. Our means can change over the course of our lifetime and can affect the choices we can afford to make. Remember, our third key message is that ***meaningful work can change over time***.

The key to using the societal factor to make your work meaningful is to think about how it is impacting you currently. Sometimes we hold on too long to old influences such as our parents' view, or don't realise we actually do have the means now to chase a dream long ago forgotten. If you are truly thinking about making work meaningful don't discount this aspect. It may be the one that turns your life completely on its head, but if it's important to you, it could be the very thing that helps you find meaningful work.

CHAPTER 8

MEANINGFUL WORK PERSONAL QUEST: *Matthew Sampson*

Matthew Sampson is the Managing Director of Aspect Personnel, a company he founded. He is the Finance Director of the Board of the Recruitment, Consulting and Staffing Association of Australia and New Zealand and he is a Structural Engineering Recruiter. He is incredibly well respected in our profession, and a thoroughly decent chap. After only two years in recruitment, he boldly set up on his own, so safe to say, he has high levels of drive and ambition. I reached out to Matt to ask if I could interview him for this book, and what he shared rang true to the theory. This is his story.

Matt boarded at Ivanhoe Grammar School in Victoria and had quite a traditional education there. On leaving school he wanted to study media and communications, but his dad, having come from a strong corporate background, suggested that first doing a Bachelor of Commerce would prove more useful. In Matt's words it was all the 'traditional middle-class English advice, you know, something safe that I could always fall back on'. So, he started studying Commerce at Melbourne University and did a number of subjects which, at the time, he couldn't stand, such as accounting, macro and microeconomics, and quantitative statistics. While he always loved spreadsheets, he really couldn't stand economic theory. Ironically now he finds it fascinating, probably because he sees the practicality of it, but at the time it was all just theory to him.

What he did start to fall in love with was the HR and marketing side of things, and that's what he ended up majoring in. In his final year at university, his elder brother and some of his friends were working in recruitment, so he had a thorough understanding as to what recruitment involved. As a result, in a move that was unusual for the time, he actively sought it out as a career.

SOCIOLOGICAL FACTORS AND CAREER CHOICES

Before we move onto Matt's entry into a career in recruitment, let's reflect for a moment on how the sociological factors here impacted his career choices. Firstly, Matt was in a fortunate position to have had a good education, both secondary and tertiary, to allow him options. Secondly, he had influences from those around him, as many do in their younger years, as to his choice of degree and further choice of career after graduation. In the first instance, the influence was against a personal choice, and in the second towards a choice that others had already made.

Through a friend, Matt ended up interviewing with Hays in his final semester for a part-time resourcing job sourcing architects, and was successful in securing the role. He was meant to be working 14 hours a week there, but ended up working the best part of 38 hours a week, squeezing in whatever he could around his studies, because he found it so enjoyable, even addictive. He finished his final exam at Melbourne University on a Friday afternoon and started full time as an Associate Consultant with Hays on the following Monday, moving into their engineering recruitment team.

Matt spent two years with Hays. He absolutely loved it. He went from an Associate Consultant to a Senior Consultant to a Manager of a team specialising in temporary recruitment. He really enjoyed the accelerated career path, a real benefit that comes with a large company like Hays. He loved working with an organisation that had others he could learn from and an organisational strategy with business plans that allowed him to grow as an individual. And he was doing the two key things which, to this day, he loves to do the most, which was recruit and lead people.

AN EVOLVING JOURNEY

As we saw in the research, the path to meaningful work is an evolving journey that is unique to each individual. This was also ringing true for Matt. He was beginning to find that his personal needs for purpose were changing. Where initially Hays's size had provided him with a sense of significance through his career path, it was becoming the very thing that was hindering his ability to continue to find meaning in his role. To maintain a sense of meaning, Matt increasingly wanted to individualise his service to his clients and candidates, and he wanted to tailor the recognition and rewards for his team members. Such customisation is, understandably, very difficult within the constraints of a large organisation and this was causing a point of tension for Matt.

This was really tough because he loved Hays. He loved what they'd taught him, the career path they'd given him, and he was excited by the career pathway he was on. He could stay there and have an excellent corporate career, and in many ways this would have met his needs for meaningful work. Here he was, only two years into his recruitment career – was he crazy to even be thinking about leaving?

Matt was having a really good, hard think about it all. It was a tough, life-changing moment for him. The thing that was crystal clear for Matt was: it wasn't about there being a problem with Hays – he wasn't going to leave them for another organisation. Swapping out Hays for another recruitment company wasn't the solution. Further, it wasn't the job – he knew he liked recruitment. But, on an individual level, Matt was wrestling with his personal narrative around work – did he want the corporate career that Hays could offer? Or did he want to be able to individualise his service and leadership and, if so, was the only way to do that to set up on his own? And could he really do that at the tender age of 22 with only two years' experience?

'I'M ALL IN, OR NOT AT ALL'

Ultimately, Matt decided to go for it. He resigned on a Monday, waited out his gardening leave, borrowed a not insignificant sum of money, and had spent 90 per cent of it before the doors of Aspect had opened. Looking back, he reflects he would do so much differently, but, with the naivety of youth and the mentality of 'I'm all in, or not at all', he rented a 108-metre square office, paid for fit out, got laptops, Blackberry phones, the whole show. He describes the way he was brought up as 'you perform to what you require', so he figured if he spent a big chunk of money, he'd have to make the business successful. He hired a receptionist and another consultant from day one. He did not wait until he had enough business to take on staff, he took the staff on to force himself to make the business successful.

The first six months were good. Matt's first couple of years' experience in recruitment were in the glory years just prior to the global financial crisis, as were the first few months of Aspect Personnel. Then the GFC hit, and everything changed. Like most recruitment firms during the GFC, business dried up for Aspect during 2009, and a number of staff resigned to pursue alternative careers. There was some concern about the long-term prospects of the business. Matt tells the story of one person, Tim, upon whom the entire business was relying at one point to accept a job offer, to get them through the next month of the GFC as things had become that tight. Fortunately, he took the job and Aspect carried on. After that, the business grew back to a staff of mid-20s and has hovered around that size consistently for the last five years.

After the Covid lockdowns Matt announced on social media that he was back on the tools, recruiting day-to-day. I was particularly interested in why Matt had stepped back from managing the business; why after running it so successfully for 15 years he decided to make a shift in what he chose to do with his time in the business. His answer to this question fascinated me. It goes to the heart of meaningful work.

While the business has been hovering around the same numbers in terms of employees for some time, prior to Covid they were a stronger business than they had ever been. For Matt, profit is about the freedom it gives you, and the purpose it allows you to achieve. It allows you to do what is important to you. In Matt's words: 'I'm happy if I can order from the left side, not the right side of the menu.' He doesn't aspire to be rich, but he does aspire to have freedom of choice and he wants that same freedom for his organisation and the people within it.

For the last few years Matt has felt like some of his decision-making capability has been constrained, and that, for him, is not meaningful work. He reflected on the fact that he was doing three roles in the organisation. He was the managing director, the board, and he is the majority shareholder. This meant he had full operational responsibility as the managing director, full risk and governance responsibility as the sole director/board, and a significant financial responsibility as the majority shareholder. He felt that this was perhaps too many hats, and he was spending too much time trying to satisfy the requirements of each role. When he reflected on what he's good at, and what he enjoys, he went back to the thing he loved, which was, and always has been, recruiting; helping candidates find jobs; working with clients and helping them succeed in their goals. What he didn't find meaningful, and in fact the key reason he had left Hays, was decisions that came about due to commercial realities. Nothing wrong with those commercial realities, they are just not Matt's own personal definition of meaningful work.

So, Matt worked with his team to create a new role for someone who could take charge of those commercials; who could work with Matt to build the budget; work with Matt to lead the strategy and the management of the recruiters to deliver that budget; free Matt up to do some bigger-picture thinking and some more hands-on recruitment. This means more leadership and recruitment, less management and commercials for Matt. Back to the stuff that always was meaningful to him.

I asked Matt to tell me about the time when he was most happy at work, and what it was about that job that made it meaningful. Interestingly, he told me about one of his first jobs, which was as a forklift driver at a warehouse in Richmond. A very different job to the career he ended up in, but what made Matt most happy with this was working in the warehouse at night to get everything spotless, everything neat and tidy. He loved the satisfaction of being given a task to do, completing it and having a sense of achievement, a sense of someone relying on him and not letting them down.

He says he still gets that same level of satisfaction today from a client entrusting him to solve a problem they have.

He describes his least favourite part of a job as when he says, 'Yes, I can solve your problem', and the inherent worry that perhaps he can't. He gets nervous about that, even now, but the most satisfying and favourite part of his job is when he does a job well, when the faith others have in him pays off. When he gets positive feedback from others on this aspect, he finds it deeply satisfying.

He told me a story of a candidate he recently placed. This candidate didn't even know the job Matt had placed him in existed, and yet, it was his dream job. As Matt said, that's the stuff that gets him out of bed! It's a pursuit of that feeling. It's really telling that his feeling of meaningful work was the same when he was a forklift driver as it is in his own recruitment company. In this example, it's not about the job, or the organisation necessarily, but about how Matt has shaped the work and adapted the job to give him the feeling that makes the work meaningful for him.

THE FLIPSIDE

I was interested, in contrast, to know perhaps when Matt had been unhappy in work, and he shared two stories.

The first was about a time when he had to fire someone. And as anyone who has had to fire someone – and who is also a human being who cares about others – knows, this is a truly difficult thing to do. It's a great example of how Matt struggles with some of the commercial necessities of his role, and how, for him, these aspects do not provide meaningful work. Matt had no choice but to fire the person for gross misconduct, to protect the organisation. It was the right thing to do – but that can be a very tough day at work.

The second time really goes to the heart of how meaningful work can change over time, particularly as our priorities change, and particularly as life events change. Matt grew up with a father who had a very strong work ethic. His dad was a senior executive in an international consumer goods company who travelled half the year and worked 12 hours or more each day, so it was normalised for Matt to have that expectation of the male role model within the family. Matt started Aspect quite a bit before he had his own family and put his heart and soul into it. It was almost hardwired into him that he would put *everything* into his business. He considered it very normal that he would work hard and make all the sacrifices now, to set him and his family up to have freedom and enjoyment later in life. When his first daughter was born, he took only one-and-a-half days off. When his son was born, he rested on his laurels, taking a week off!

Matt wouldn't have described himself as unhappy at the time, he was driven by a societal factor, his upbringing, and he thought he was doing the right thing by his family in setting them up for the future. That drive and the success the business was enjoying was fulfilling at the time.

Then Covid happened, and spending so much time with his family (or in his brilliant choice of words, 'supercharging his time with his family') made him really, really realise what he was actually sacrificing by not being with them. Matt was in Melbourne for Covid, in one of the longest lockdowns in the world. That experience made Matt think about today as well as the future, and reflect on trying to find a better balance. It made him think about how he could make his work more meaningful now. Matt describes Covid as a breather from an escalating cycle he was on. Looking back, he realised perhaps he wasn't as fulfilled as he thought. It allowed him to pause and reflect in a way that he doesn't think he would have been able to do if it hadn't happened.

CHAPTER 9
MEANINGFUL WORK CHANGES OVER TIME

WHAT HAS CHANGED FOR YOU OVER TIME?

When we consider the factors of meaningful work, we really start to see how it can be so challenging to find, retain and provide meaningful work. If you've read this far, you have a comprehensive understanding that:

- everyone's path to meaningful work is unique
- there are four factors of meaningful work: individual, job, organisational and societal.

This brings us to the third and final key message:

- **Measuring meaningful work is the key to finding and providing it, especially because it can change over time.**

When our academics conducted a research review they found that all prior studies had focused only on the current state of meaningful work for the individual, but failed to take into consideration an ideal state or desired future state. Prior research had failed to review how meaningful work can change over time.

Yet, when we think about meaningful work, we all intrinsically know that it changes over time. If you're doubting that, let me ask you a question: what was your first ever paid job? Did you find it meaningful, and if so, why? Or conversely, why not? I ask this question every time I deliver a keynote or facilitate a workshop on meaningful work. Typically, the answers tend to be jobs such as babysitting, newspaper rounds, working in a local shop or helping out with the family business. More often than not, people found their first jobs meaningful. Usually, they loved the sense of independence, they enjoyed earning money for the first time and sometimes, if they were lucky, they also actually enjoyed the work they were doing. When this happens, I hear statements such as:

- 'Working in the shop, I loved the interaction with the customers and using my brain to work out the change needed.'
- 'When babysitting, I loved playing with the kids, and as a plus when they went to bed, I felt like I was getting paid to do my homework.'
- 'I enjoyed the physical activity of doing my paper round, enjoyed being outside and liked the quiet.'

When people *didn't* find their first job meaningful it's often because they didn't find something in it that matched their individual factors. I go on to ask, would you find that job meaningful today? And the answer is usually no. When this happens, I hear statements such as:

- 'I still enjoy dealing with customers but working in a shop, now, wouldn't give me the intellectual stimulation I enjoy.'
- 'I need to do more than sit in someone's house, and babysitting wouldn't pay enough for my current needs.'
- 'I still love doing a job that is physical, but would need to do something with greater outcomes than delivering a paper.'

As you've read these examples, you've likely been thinking about your first job and whether it was meaningful and would it still be now. If you haven't already, take a moment to think about it. It's really interesting to reflect on which aspects of meaning haven't changed, and it can be useful to assess whether you are getting enough of those aspects of meaningful work in your current job. It's also useful to assess what has changed over time and why. This will help you as you move forward and, as your circumstances change and evolve, it will help you to consider what might change next to keep you in meaningful work.

One of the best things about meaningful work and how it changes is how often in retirement and semi-retirement people can go back to what they found meaningful earlier in their life. I knew someone whose first job was as a swim instructor and who has every intention of returning to that in semi-retirement, following a professional corporate career.

Take some time now to consider how meaningful work has changed over time for you.

What was your first paid job?

_____

What aspects of that job were meaningful?
Think about the individual, job, organisational and societal factors.

_____

What aspects of that job were not meaningful?
Think about the individual, job, organisational and societal factors.

_____

For the factors that were meaningful, are there any that are still meaningful for you today that are missing in your current role, and if so how could you try to incorporate them into your work?

_____

Jot some notes down, from reflecting on this exercise, about how meaningful work has changed for you over time.

_____

CHAPTER 10
MEANINGFUL WORK PERSONAL QUEST: *Mimi Naylor*

Mimi Naylor is the Founder and Clinical Director of Talkshop Speech Pathology, a private speech pathology practice based in Sydney with three centres, which also provides telehealth services Australia-wide and overseas. Mimi's story of meaningful work is fascinating for a number of reasons. She has worked within large bureaucratic systems such as hospitals and universities, as well as within private practice; she works within a hands-on health-based industry, and her experience is from the UK, India and Australia. Like many people who work in allied health, her profile isn't full of details of a personal nature, and it isn't full of her own successes. Her drivers of meaningful work aren't easy to guess at from reading her profile. She is an ADHDer and proudly neurodiverse, so proud she prefers identity-first language rather than person-first language. I wanted to interview Mimi as someone who might represent a different segment of the drivers of meaningful work, and, as with the other personal stories, was delighted to find when I interviewed her there was more depth to her journey than I could have hoped for. I'm sure you'll agree.

Mimi's first role was as a volunteer 'tea girl' at age 16 in a residential care home in the UK. She walked around each floor pushing the tea trolley offering tea, coffee and cold drinks. In what was perhaps symbolic of what might become meaningful work for Mimi, an incident happened in her first couple of days on this job. As she was doing her rounds, she saw an elderly gentleman who appeared to have been sitting in his armchair all day with no mobility. This struck her, and she got talking with him. Mimi is a very extroverted, chatty person. You get the sense that she is happy to talk with anyone. She felt for this man, and she wanted to help him; another strong driver for Mimi for meaningful work.

She didn't like the fact he was 'stuck' in his chair, and she is a very action-oriented person. So, she sat on the floor with him and talked about the importance of staying active even when he was sitting. She devised activities for him to lift his legs, and to strengthen and stretch his muscles. She recalls that as she was on the floor with this gentleman and they were excitedly celebrating just how high he could lift his leg, which by the way was only about 30 centimetres off the ground, out of the corner of her eye she caught a glimpse of the charge nurse passing by. Shortly after, Mimi was summoned to see the nurse, admonished and quickly relinquished of her volunteer role.

As an adult now, Mimi understands that, despite her good intentions, she was no physiotherapist and this impulsively devised exercise plan was completely out of her remit. While her tea-girl job abruptly finished up as a result of this incident, Mimi's empathic connection, desire to help others and the drive for action were there from the beginning. Those three aspects of meaningful work have stayed with her through her career. Thankfully she has learnt how to better channel her strengths.

THE ACCIDENTAL SPEECH PATHOLOGIST

At university Mimi accidentally studied speech pathology. Living in England at the time, as a child of refugees she had grown up speaking three languages at home. When reviewing the university course handbook, it flipped open onto speech and language therapy. She didn't really know what speech pathology was but assumed it was to do with languages, so thought it might be well-suited to her given her language skills. It also met the criteria of studying something 'useful', having previously been told by her dad that her interest in photography should be pursued as a hobby. With no research into the course or the profession, she applied to a top-tier London university and was accepted. She quickly discovered the course had nothing to do with languages. Further, Mimi hadn't done any prerequisite subjects. She found the time at university unexpectedly hard, even though living in London as a student had many social upsides.

Through university, all of her casual jobs maximised her extroverted, people-loving nature and desire to help. She worked as a nursing assistant in a care home, this time staying within the remit of her role. She worked for Thames Water, going door to door in London persuading people to sign up for and pay their water rates. Like many, she also worked as a waitress, and recalls illogical instances where she was retained as a waitress due to her 'people skills' despite her disastrous table-serving skills. She recounts a time when, serving at Henley Royal Regatta, she accidentally spilled half a bottle of wine down the back of a patron's jacket. Another instance she remembers was while working at the Eurofighter tent at the Paris Air Show, her entire team, except her, were sacked for 'poor service', even though she had just caused a mountain of peas to cascade across the tent, due to her picking up a hot dish and burning her fingers. She worked as 'Front of House' in a boutique hotel in Hampstead, cheerfully managing customer complaints about the lack of hot water, which she knew would never be fixed in such an old building. She also worked in a London call centre doing market research, cold calling companies in Hong Kong and Australia, often talking with Managers and CEOs who 'just liked to have a good conversation'. We can see Mimi was honing her people skills through this time.

Her first job as a speech and language therapist after university was at a large teaching hospital in Poole, Dorset. She lived in the nurses' accommodation. Mimi was in a rotational position, starting on the general medical wards, then the acute stroke unit, and then in brain injury rehabilitation. It was quite an introduction to the world of speech pathology. She found the brain injury rehab fascinating because it is what is known as 'slow stream', which provides the opportunity for patients to get gradual rehabilitation through incremental adjustments in their programmes, tailored to their needs. The clients Mimi was working with on this ward had significant trauma, ranging from road accidents to assault, to even, at the time, Creutzfeldt-Jakob disease (Mad Cow Disease). She learnt a lot in this ward, but equally loved the fast pace of the general medical ward and the stroke unit.

She loved the work; she loved the hospital. Some of the key things for her – interacting with others, helping people, action orientation – were being met. She did this role for two years. One thing, however, was causing it to be problematic. She was having a very difficult time, from a relationship perspective, with a direct manager. She had a great relationship with all her peers, but this one manager, who had a lot of influence, was making life very difficult.

During this time, her boyfriend had moved to Australia, so she left to do some travelling in Australia and to see him. When she returned, she went back to work in another brain injury rehabilitation facility, which she did for two years, to save enough money to marry her, by now, fiancé, and for them to move to Australia permanently.

Mimi moved to Australia in 2006 and started in a series of locum positions. She found it hard to secure a permanent position in Sydney. She believes this is because speech pathology is predominantly a female profession, resulting in a public health system with few permanent positions available, with many roles being short-term maternity cover. This also coincided with 'The Agenda for Change', the largest ever attempt to introduce a new pay system in the UK public services, covering more than one million National Health Service staff.[29] This meant that many working holiday Australian speech pathology locums returned to Australia in this period. As a result, Mimi worked in these locum positions for a number of years, while also having her own children.

It was at this point that the University of Sydney contacted Mimi to ask if she would work with them as an Associate Lecturer and Clinical Educator. Mimi had previously supervised their students at Bankstown-Lidcombe Hospital as a Clinical Educator. This would be a similar role but with the university as the employer. She supervised undergraduate third- and fourth-year students and master's students, and lectured in Clinical Case Management and Ethics.

Despite the fact that she had been thinking about launching something on her own, Mimi jumped at the opportunity. It met her needs for meaningful work on so many levels. She really couldn't imagine a better job than helping develop students to become their absolute best. Ironically, Mimi's unpleasant encounter with the manager in her first hospital job paved the way for her to create more meaningful work in this university role. She set out to empower her students with confidence and to build their clinical expertise, hoping to help them avoid the difficulties she herself had faced. For the longest time this was enough for Mimi. For six years she devoted herself to this job,

---

29   www.ncbi.nlm.nih.gov/pmc/articles/PMC2475534/

describing it as one of the most rewarding experiences in her professional journey.

THE NEXT STEP

Meaningful work though, as the research tells us, changes over time. And so it was for Mimi. There were two things that made Mimi realise she needed to take that next step in her meaningful work journey. Both are linked to the challenges that come from working within the confines of a large system.

The first comes back to her action orientation that is in Mimi's DNA. The very thing that made her sit on the floor with the old gentleman in the care home and want to stretch out his legs. Mimi started to get increasingly frustrated by her lack of ability to create change. If Mimi has an idea that is really exciting, and fun to do, she really wants to do it, ideally now! Whereas universities plan their programmes far in advance. Semester one, semester two, all the units, all the components done many months earlier, and often a year or more ahead of time. Mimi reflects that if you have an idea, it's difficult to make the change until maybe semester two of the following year, and even then, it's likely to be a pilot study, which then has to be reviewed and evaluated.

The second challenge Mimi faced was again a conflict of leadership. Mimi had a disagreement with some senior academics over whether some students were ready to graduate. While Mimi was expressing her concerns, she had some frustrations with how those concerns were being listened to. Her feelings of frustration grew alongside the new child in her belly and she started to revisit her entrepreneurial ideas, and what meaningful work was to her now.

With the birth of her third child, she set out on a completely new endeavour.

There are not many people who would think about giving up secure employment with a university, when they have three young children, to set up their own business unless they are financially independent. You may well think that Mimi was lucky enough to have a level of security, allowing her to consider an entrepreneurial idea at this stage of her life. Before we explore this, I'd like to share with you some of the societal factors that have influenced her journey.

Mimi is the daughter of refugees. Her parents left Vietnam for England, arriving in 1979 with nothing. Even once Mimi's parents had settled in England, every spare penny they earned they would send back to the family. As a result, Mimi has a very ambivalent attitude towards money and possessions. She doesn't feel like she has to hold on to things, and she feels that if someone else needs something, they can have it. This background has also given her an incredible strength and resilience. She remembers 'sliding down the wall in the kitchen' worrying about it, but thinking to herself, *if my Mum and Dad can leave as refugees, go across the water to an unknown land and hope for a better future, if they have that strength and resilience, I have that as part of my DNA.* That helped Mimi.

The other societal factor that has had a compelling impact on meaningful work for Mimi is her faith. Mimi describes herself as a 'Jesus follower', discovering a richly fulfilling spiritual life for herself as a young adult, although she was raised in the Christian faith. Mimi often talks about the 'constant space of fear' she feels at work, worrying that she is not doing enough and not achieving enough, which she thinks is likely related to her ADHD, where she needs to be constantly 'on the go'. She feels lost if she's not multi-tasking, juggling a thousand things. She experiences this as a steady pressure, and she talks of her spirit always praying for 'her eyes to see and her heart to carry'. The way she sees it, God is the Creator of everything, and the most creative genius, so she often thinks to herself, 'This is really His work-place.' Her spirit simply asks for a divine download of creativity and guidance in perceiving situations and decisions. When the pressure is intense, or whenever she is unsure, she simply asks God with an open heart, 'Help me see with your eyes, what do you need me to do?'

These are great examples of how societal factors can shape our work choices. Often the societal factor is about means and access to meaningful work. We sometimes review it in terms of how it has limited our choices, but in Mimi's case it's a great example of how others' determination, and her faith, opened up a whole new world of possibilities.

Let's now look at where these possibilities have taken her. While on maternity leave in 2014, Mimi had the time to revisit some of her earlier themes of meaningful work, particularly her desire to be entrepreneurial. She undertook a small business management course in the evenings through TAFE, and after returning to the university to complete her six-month contract, she started a small private speech pathology practice.

GOING IT ALONE

Initially, she hired a tiny room within an occupational therapy service. She tells me, fondly, it was 'basically a storeroom for chairs and files and things, not practical at all'. The other thing she did from the get-go was set up a drop-in clinic in their local library with free speech pathology consultations, to build up a bit of a waitlist so that when she was ready to officially launch, she already had a potential client list. A sign of that entrepreneurial spirit.

Mimi had her little practice in that OT room for less than six months; it was so tiny that they often had to run their sessions in the corridor. When describing this she actually said, 'we basically had to play in the corridor'. It's true she predominately treats children, and she uses a lot of play-based therapy, but the fact that she uses the word 'play', rather than 'treat', or 'have clinics', or any other choice of language she could use, I think tells you a lot about how meaningful she finds this work. Most of the time they were running up and down the corridor. They were located right next to a lawyer's office. When Mimi came back from their Christmas break there were multiple signs up saying, 'No noise' and 'No running in the corridor'. Mimi, with her positive mindset, took this as a sign that she needed to find a bigger office space and move out.

The first real premises she had of her own was five rooms, and she made all the mistakes that new business owners make. Her main one was around collecting money. Having worked for the NHS in the UK and then for big organisations like hospitals and universities here in Australia, she had no idea how to collect money. Her first invoices were done as Word documents, and she'd email them and think to herself 'it might be nice if they'd pay', and then just leave it, hoping for the best!

The business grew and it got to the point where she needed to take on her first employee, a contractor, to help out. However, she had all these outstanding invoices, and hadn't been paying herself a proper wage, so she had to borrow money from her husband's salary to pay her first contractor's wage. It was a very steep learning curve, despite having done the business management course. This was less about the process itself, and more about her personal boundaries and her comfort levels with talking to people about these areas. She was learning and growing, despite the levels of discomfort that were coming with it.

More than anything, she was driven to create a team and a place where people could feel completely nurtured and fully supported in their profession. The aspects of meaningful work for Mimi that hadn't changed were the development of others, helping others, as well as that action orientation. These were coming together in a way that was driving her to build and create something truly spectacular. What she wanted, and how she describes her practice, Talkshop, was to create something that was really fun and different; that has a culture that is open and honest; where the team can go hard to learn, fail and pick themselves up; where mistakes are okay, because we all learn through them; where play is a big part of what they do every day. When I interviewed Mimi, Talkshop had grown to 12 speech pathologists, and this is how she feels about the work she and the team do there: 'I just love everything about it. I love the people. And I love that we're always dreaming and I feel like everybody pulls their weight, in that we're all aligned together because we all dream the same dream.'

PART II
THE
MEANINGFUL
WORK PROFILE
TOOL

CHAPTER 11
THE INDIVIDUAL MEANINGFUL WORK PROFILE TOOL

Phew. That's a lot to take in, right? It's no wonder so many people struggle in their quest to find meaningful work, and why so many organisations struggle to provide meaningful work, despite their best efforts.

Well, the good news is, we've simplified it for you. We knew that to help people understand all this complex theory and find a way to practically use this information, we needed to design a tool for individuals to measure meaningful work, hence the Individual Meaningful Work Profile Tool, or MWPT, was born.

THE INDIVIDUAL MWPT

We have developed a new fit-for-purpose tool that overcomes the significant limitations of the existing tools, and adequately captures the full breadth of those four factors of meaningful work (individual, job, organisation and societal).[30] The MWPT makes no assumptions

---

30   The tool was validated against survey responses from a predominantly Australian audience (97%).

about the importance of meaningful work for you as an individual, and it is future focused, because you can take it as often as you want as your circumstances change. Further, it is the only tool to consider both the psychological and sociological perspectives. And we have made it free and available for anyone to use anywhere.[31]

WHAT DOES IT MEASURE?

The MWPT has been built using existing behavioural-based research by constructing statements against the four factors of meaningful work. Remembering that there is no right or wrong, and that everyone's path to meaningful work is unique, it asks you to measure how much you agree or disagree with each statement when considering meaningful work. The trick of the tool is to really take time to reflect on your answers. With the statements being based on research, it is common when you first take the tool to agree with all of the statements, because in an ideal world we'd all have a role that incorporated every aspect of meaningful work. Considering how important each statement is to you, particularly in reference to the other statements, is key. Relatively speaking, how important do you feel the questions are and how much does that influence the degree to which you agree or disagree with each statement?

Our research also allowed us to ensure it would be fit for purpose, with it being refined to ensure consistency, reliability and validity. During the pilot study to build the tool, each statement was assessed to determine its suitability to measure meaningful work, and whether it improved the model. Those statements that didn't meet these criteria were discarded. Thus, the profile tool has been built to provide you with an analysis of the factors of meaningful work meeting the standard statistical measures of internal consistency, reliability, validity,

---

31   You can take your MWPT by visiting www.meaningfulwork.com.au.

and model-fit parameters. What that means, in non-academic speak, is that if not enough people found the factor meaningful, it didn't make it into the tool. That's worth remembering because, as we've said a number of times before, everyone's path to meaningful work is unique. Therefore, when using the tool, if you feel like something is missing, feel free to consider that it may still be an important factor for you as an individual.

And to give you a little taster, at a high level it looks like this:

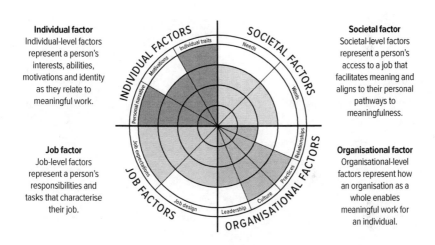

Individual factor
Individual-level factors represent a person's interests, abilities, motivations and identity as they relate to meaningful work.

Societal factor
Societal-level factors represent a person's access to a job that facilitates meaning and aligns to their personal pathways to meaningfulness.

Job factor
Job-level factors represent a person's responsibilities and tasks that characterise their job.

Organisational factor
Organisational-level factors represent how an organisation as a whole enables meaningful work for an individual.

This is my personal profile for meaningful work as it stood in February 2022, above. The top-left quadrant looks at those individual factors, broken down into the subsets of personal narrative, motivations and individual traits. The greater the shading the stronger those factors are for me. You can see from the shading the individual factors are strong overall for me, with personal narrative and individual traits being my strongest two. When you are actually in the tool online you can click in further and it gives you more detail behind each section to explain the factors and the questions you answered behind them.

The bottom-left quadrant looks at the job factor, specifically how much the job can be designed to accommodate meaningful work and the expectations (safety, fair work conditions, and how much control and career opportunities you have). Job expectations are more important to me than job design.

The bottom-right quadrant looks at the organisational factors, broken down into the subsets of leadership, culture, practices and relationships. By the shading you can see culture and practices are more important to me than leadership or relationships.

The final quadrant, at the top right, is the societal factor which represents your access to a job that aligns with your personal factors and is broken down into needs (how important is it to you that the organisation shares your values, and provides an environment where health, safety and wellbeing are a priority) and wants (needing to feel like the organisation cares about you as an individual, in different ways).

Remember how I said it can change over time? Well, here is my profile as it was in January 2023.

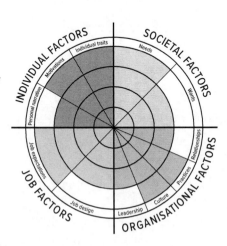

Individual factor
Individual-level factors represent a person's interests, abilities, motivations and identity as they relate to meaningful work.

Job factor
Job-level factors represent a person's responsibilities and tasks that characterise their job.

Societal factor
Societal-level factors represent a person's access to a job that facilitates meaning and aligns to their personal pathways to meaningfulness.

Organisational factor
Organisational-level factors represent how an organisation as a whole enables meaningful work for an individual.

WHAT CAN IT TELL YOU?

Let's examine my February 2022 profile, so that when you complete the MWPT you have a good understanding of what it is telling you. If you haven't yet taken your own MWPT you can do so by visiting www.meaningfulwork.com.au. (You'll need about 10 to 15 minutes of uninterrupted time to think it through properly and give it the consideration it deserves.) If you can, while you're reading through this, it's a good idea to have your own profile open on the screen and hover over the relevant section of your wheel as it will help you see how I have interpreted the information.

Individual factors

We'll start with the individual factors in the top-left quadrant. Remember, these are the factors of meaningful work that are about me as an individual, my interests, abilities, personality traits, motives and goals. If you think about those aspects of yourself and then look at your results here you can start to tie the two together.

On personal narrative we can see that work is a very important part of who I am and how I see myself, and I need to be doing work that aligns with my self-identity and provides me with a sense of accomplishment. Knowing that this is a very strong factor of meaningful work for me allows me to think about that further: what is my self-identity around work? What does self-accomplishment look like for me?

The other very strong individual factor is my individual traits – I need work that allows me to be high performing and work to my strengths and gives me a blend of teamwork and working autonomously. All true and useful to know when thinking about the balance of duties within my role.

It is interesting to note, however, that these factors are stronger than my motivations subset. In February 2022 the motivations subset of the individual factor was not as strong as it was by January 2023, which switched in levels of importance with personal narrative. I can tell you that, after all the lockdowns, by February 2022, it was absolutely the personal identity that I had around work that kept me going, rather than my individual motivation at that point in time. It was contributing to outcomes that made a difference to others that motivated me more than any personal individual motivation. This is one of the ways in which lockdowns affected my results. I'll share the other ways as we continue to talk through my profile.

Job factors

The second factor we'll look at is the job factor. If I am on the website, I'll be able to see by hovering over this factor that it is less important to me that my job is recognised by others, but it is more important that work conditions are safe, that I have control over my approach to work, and opportunities to develop my career. This is one part that didn't change for me at all as a result of the lockdowns, so it seems I'm consistent in this regard!

Organisational factors

Let's turn to the organisational factors. These represent how the organisation, as a whole, enables meaningful work for an individual.

There are some interesting things to note on my profile tool here. The first is that, in February 2022, relationships is my lowest factor of meaningful work across my whole profile. This means that working in a social environment is less important for me. There are two things about this that are worth exploring. One internally focused. One externally.

Let's take the external focus first. We touched on this already when we explored the organisational factor of meaningful work. Having friendships and social engagement at work is a highly popular factor of meaningful work. It shows up again and again in various pieces of research to improve outcomes. For example, those who have a best friend at work are twice as likely to be engaged in their jobs, be better at engaging customers, produce higher quality work and have a greater sense of wellbeing and are less likely to get injured on the job.[32] For this reason, many engagement and culture surveys ask questions about social environment at work, and then make assumptions as to how that relates to positive engagement and culture. They are not wrong to do so; it is a statistically valid thing to do. But for me, as an individual, it isn't very relevant. This takes us back to the very first key message: everyone's path to meaningful work is unique.

The second interesting fact about this aspect of meaningful work is internal. When I reflect on why my score is low it tells me a lot about how the factors of meaningful work can change over time. Thinking about my career, there have absolutely been times when having friends at work was crucial for it to be meaningful, particularly when I was younger. In fact, I met my husband through a friend at work (thanks Nic!). But as I've got older and my role has grown, I have more responsibilities both in and out of work, and I struggle to stay on top of the relationships I have. I know through my Strengths Profile I am a relationship deepener, meaning I like to have deep, ongoing relationships with those close to me. I feel the weight of the responsibility of not being able to give as much as I would like to those close friends. So, I don't have a need to add extra relationships to that. I love to be friendly at work, I love to socialise with people at work, I love spending time with people at work, but at this point in my life and career I don't *need* it for my work to be meaningful.

What's interesting to note though is that this factor did change as a result of coming out of lockdown. It didn't go up enough to be one of

---

32   Gallup (2018), 'Why we need best friends at work'.

my most dominant factors, the points I make above are still relevant, but clearly being in lockdown had an impact on how important I felt relationships were to me, and coming out of lockdown did increase the level of importance of them. I now understand, from being back in the office and spending time in person with people at work again, the importance of those relationships is heightened, and I value that more now having experienced it again. When I was withdrawn from it during lockdown, it was easier to underestimate the importance of it too.

This really does remind us of our third key message: measuring meaningful work is the key to finding and providing it, especially because it can change over time.

Moving round the MWPT, you can see that culture and practices are crucial to me for meaningful work. I need to work for an organisation that makes a difference in people's lives and cares about giving back to the community, and I need a culture that has enough creativity to allow me to work without constraint. All the things I love about my job now!

Societal factors

Onto the societal factors, remembering that these factors represent my ability to access a job that facilitates meaning and aligns with my personal pathways to meaningfulness. This is something that doesn't generally come up as strongly for me. It's somewhat important to me that the organisation I work for shares my values, creates a safe and wellbeing-focused environment and cares for me as an individual, but in February 2022 they weren't my driving factors of meaningful work.

However, by January 2023 something had changed. You can see the 'needs' subset of the societal factor has become a dominant factor of meaningful work by this point. On the website, I can hover over this subset and see that this means I need my organisation to share in creating an environment where health, safety and wellbeing are a priority. Typically, while I appreciate a lot of people love this factor, personally I'm quite comfortable to manage my own health and wellbeing and this is not something I think of as the organisation's responsibility, beyond ensuring it meets its legal obligation. I suspect that this change came about off the back of the busiest year I've ever experienced in my career. Record unemployment combined with opening up after lockdown and many organisations turbocharging all their plans after the Covid years of being on hold meant I had worked harder in the preceding months than I had ever worked. This is likely what drove the change in my profile.

* * *

As you consider these areas you can start thinking about how all these factors impact your career, either when looking for work or when trying to progress or develop your current role. Are all four quadrants for meaningful work being met? If not, what could you do to try to improve that?

Hopefully as I've gone around the wheel of my MWPT, you have done the same with yours and it has started you thinking about what your tool tells you about yourself. It's a great exercise to do with someone else too, even as a team activity, so you can really start to think about how you create more opportunities for meaningful work, for yourself and for others.

How can you use the Meaningful Work Profile Tool?

You can use and interpret your report in several ways. You can look at your wheel, and through your additional understanding that you've gleaned in this book, you can think about what it tells you about yourself and your work. Remember, meaningful work is unique, and this is about **you**. Did any of the information surprise you? Did you have any 'a-ha' moments?

Consider re-taking the MWPT if your wheel is quite 'full'; that is, every quadrant is full of colour or very near full of colour. This is very common the first time someone does their profile, because you are being asked about how important the factors of meaningful work are … and all those factors are nice to haves. To get an MWPT that will be truly useful, deeply consider your answers, and spend some time weighing up, relatively speaking, how important each factor is. Try to suppress the urge to tick 'strongly agree, strongly agree, strongly agree'.

You can also talk your results over with someone: a trusted friend or family member, a colleague, your boss. You can even contact us to have a professional coaching session around your profile if you want an in-depth view of your data. Your MWPT is personal to you, reflecting back your data to assess the ways in which you currently find work meaningful. Due to the fact it changes over time, you can re-take it as many times as you like.

It is what you do with this information that makes this potentially life changing. So, let's delve into the two main ways you might use it personally:

- developing your fulfilment and career potential within your current role
- jobseeking for an entirely new position.

Using the MWPT in your current role

If you've read through this book in order, you'll probably already have taken some notes in the exercises sections that will help you in conjunction with your MWPT. Now think about the questions below while looking at your MWPT. *The trick is in looking at which factors are meaningful for you in your MWPT that perhaps you aren't currently experiencing within your own role.* I don't recommend spending too much time thinking about how to improve the factors that are, relatively speaking, less meaningful to you, or those that are high but in which you are already happy.

Once you've identified a relevant factor you wish to improve upon, try to articulate specifically what it is about that factor you would like to see change, that would help it align with your need for meaning in these areas. This will give you a way to see if you can adapt your current role or work with your leaders or organisation to help improve that area. An additional benefit is that if this factor becomes more meaningful for you, it's likely to help others too. You might, for instance, talk to your boss about your next steps and what they might look like. Or it might be that you need to work on understanding how some of the societal factors are influencing you and whether that's in conflict with your individual ones.

Consider these questions:

Individual:

Are you able to enjoy using your interests in your current role?

_____

Are you able to use your capabilities or strengths in your current role?

_____

Is your current role meeting your goals for the next three years?

_____

Does your current role align with the story you tell yourself about the importance of work?

_____

Job:

Are your work conditions meeting or exceeding your expectations?

_____

How much are you able to design or modify your job to enable more meaning?

_____

Organisation:

Is your current leadership inspiring you?

_____

Do you know what the organisational goals are and how you are contributing towards those goals?

_____

Does your current culture get the best out of you?

_____

How important are your current working relationships to you?

_____

What do the practices of your organisation mean to you?

_____

Societal:

Are you ever under pressure in your current role from family or friends to either stay even though you dislike it, or leave even though you love it?

_____

Do you hold off telling your family or friends about potential promotions or opportunities at work out of concern about how they may react?

_____

Do you feel your current organisation isn't looking after your health, safety and wellbeing and yet you expect that they should, or conversely do they put a lot of effort into this space and you find it somewhat odd that they do?

_____

Does your organisation take an interest in your personal development and career fulfillment, and do you expect that of them?

_____

How do your answers to these questions make you feel about your current job?

_____

To put this exercise in context, for a substantial part of my early career I thought I wanted to be a teacher. I grew up in a culture that very much valued teachers. I had a huge appreciation for how some specific teachers significantly influenced my life for the better when I was a troubled teenager (thank you Mr Reynolds, Mrs Rodgers). I have strengths in explaining things and enjoying helping others to achieve. In many ways it would have met my needs for meaningful work.

However, because I wasn't 100 per cent sure this is what I wanted to do, I did my undergraduate degree first, thinking I would do a teacher conversion post-graduate course if I still wanted to. But, when it came to it, I couldn't afford to. I didn't have the means to put myself through another year of university on part-time waitress wages. Instead, I entered the professional workforce full time. At a few points I toyed with going back to university to do my teacher training, but I was never willing to give up my salary to do so. As I rose in my career into leadership roles, I was increasingly able to teach others around me. I collaborated with colleagues to build in-house training, and I regularly run masterclasses and professional development sessions within our consulting practice for our clients. I've been able to adapt my job to include an element that I always wanted to do. Essentially, I've incorporated the aspects I thought I would like about teaching into the job I do, and this is one of the ways in which my work has become more meaningful.

Using the MWPT when jobseeking

Understanding how you can use the MWPT in an existing role, it becomes clearer how you might use it if you are jobseeking (or indeed if you are a leader hiring into your own team).

The process for jobseeking is similar. Looking at your MWPT, isolate the specific factors that are meaningful to you but are not currently being met. Then, reviewing the questions below, think about how you are exploring these areas in your job search. Are you asking these questions in an interview, or doing your research online or with others in the industry to establish if you are targeting the right organisations or jobs? (And, if you are hiring, are you thinking about how the job you are recruiting for and your organisation would address these areas, and are you sharing this information in your job advert and recruitment process?)

Individual:

Do the roles you are considering align with your interests?

_____

Which of your capabilities or strengths would you like to use in your next role and are you clear how you can do that in the roles you are applying for?

_____

How do the jobs you are thinking of applying to align to your personal goals for the next three years?

_____

Do the roles you are considering align with the story you tell yourself about the importance of work? If not, do you need to change the types of roles or the story you tell yourself?

_____

Job:

What kind of work conditions would meet or exceed your expectations?

_____

How much autonomy will you have to be able to design or modify the jobs you are applying for to enable more meaning?

_____

Organisation:

Is the leadership of the organisation you are applying to inspiring you?

_____

Do you know what the organisational goals are and how your potential role would contribute towards those goals?

_____

What type of culture gets the best out of you? And does it match the culture of the organisations you are applying to?

_____

How important are friendships at work for you, and could you be friends with the people you are meeting?

_____

What are the practices of your target organisation, and do they align to your needs and expectations?

_____

Societal:

What will your family, friends and social circle say about the roles you are applying for?

_____

Are there any roles or career changes you've considered but not explored for fear of what others might say?

_____

Would you consider a different career if your means or access was different, and is there an interim path that might take you there?

Does your target organisation's emphasis on your individual fulfilment, wellbeing and career align with your own expectations?

When jobseeking or considering potential career changes, the time spent thinking about these areas, and specifically how important they are to you individually, could be the very thing that leads you to life-long career fulfilment. Firstly, it could really help you to understand what has made you unhappy in the past, and what you can look for to get the balance more in your favour this time around. Secondly, it'll give you really good questions to ask in your research and in your interviews, which means you'll be a better prepared, better suited candidate and be more likely to get the role. Thirdly, the chances of picking the right role will increase, so your performance, engagement, enjoyment, retention and career development will all improve. Time taken to do this research well, now, could truly change the course of your life for the future.

CHAPTER 12

THE ORGANISATIONAL MEANINGFUL WORK PROFILE TOOL

If the Individual MWPT is our attempt to help people connect to more meaningful work, what does that mean for all of you reading this who are in leadership roles, wondering to yourselves: *How on earth do I ensure I am providing meaningful work to people? How do I create an organisation where people genuinely thrive at work? Where they love what they do? Where as many of those factors of meaningful work are maximised as possible? And how do I do that when there are so many different aspects to meaningful work?*

As we saw in our research, when an employee experiences meaningful work there are direct benefits for the organisation, therefore there is significant value for you, as a leader, to be able to establish and improve the ways in which you offer meaningful work. This is why we also built the Organisational Meaningful Work Profile Tool.

WHAT DOES IT MEASURE?

The Organisational MWPT creates organisation-focused statements influenced by the individual statements. This allows an individual within an organisation to complete the organisational tool based on the ways the organisation is currently providing meaningful work. For example, in the individual tool one of the statements is, 'I am energised when I work with others'. In the organisational tool this becomes, 'Our employees are regularly required to work with others'. In this way the organisation gets a view from every employee of how the organisation measures up against the researched areas of meaningful work.

The data is anonymised, and can be broken down by team, geography and certain demographic information. It is also customisable to allow a number of additional questions you may wish to be included for specific purposes.

In addition, the organisation can ask its employees to take the Individual MWPT so it can compare these results against the organisation profile.

WHAT CAN IT TELL YOU?

The value of the tool is in the analysis and the time spent reviewing and discussing. Remember that everyone's path to meaningful work is unique; it actually doesn't matter if, as an organisation, there are a number of areas you are not scoring highly on for meaningful work, as long as those areas are not in conflict with what your employees are looking for! The gold in this tool is the ability to go way beyond culture or engagement surveys to really dig into the aspects of your workplace that you can tweak that can make the biggest difference. You may have poor leadership practices, but if you have a team that doesn't rate leadership that highly on the meaningful work individual tool, you don't need to put that high on your list in terms of time and resources to fix.

It will tell you what you are already doing well, and you can discuss as a leadership team what you do with that information. For example, are you sharing the learnings from these areas enough? Are you using these aspects in your attraction and retention campaigns? Are there people within your organisation who can learn from these areas quickly and easily if this is something that most people are already doing well? There will be some quick wins. It will also give you some feedback on areas you may have 'had a feeling' about – it will give you the hard data to dig further, highlight a problem area or provide the information you need to take an issue to the Board, for example.

HOW CAN YOU USE IT?

The Organisational MWPT tool is best used on a regular basis, quarterly or biannually I'd recommend. It's best reviewed as part of your strategic leadership meetings. If it is not reviewed and actioned, it runs the risk of becoming like a lot of surveys that tell you things that you kinda, sorta already know but do nothing about. If you make it part of your review cycle, it could become part of your secret sauce that really does separate you from your competition.

The Organisational MWPT allows an organisation to use the regular reviews to determine which areas of meaningful work it wants to improve, strategically picking those factors it thinks may make the biggest difference to its organisation within its own sector, giving it a significant advantage over its competitors at a time of talent shortage.

To put that into perspective let me share some of the evidence that came out of our academic research which shows that meaningful work is not only good for individuals, but great for organisations too. Meaningful work has been linked to higher engagement levels, lower withdrawal intentions and rates of absenteeism, and increased employee commitment to the organisation. Meaningful work has also been found to significantly increase measurable organisational performance, even so far as strengthening and protecting an organisation's performance during downturns and downsizing.[33]

What it is that motivates you, whatever meaningful work is to you, it is likely to be for your people too, and that will be good for business. There is much evidence that supports that this is worth your time and effort to follow up on.

---

33   'Meaningful work and the development of a Meaningful Work Profiling Tool', Dr Jill Rathborne and Dr Elizabeth Shoesmith, November 2019.

CHAPTER 13

MEANINGFUL WORK PERSONAL QUEST: *Shirley Chowdhary*

Shirley Chowdhary is a Non-Executive Director, Advisory Board member and advisor. In 2019 she was named by the *Australian Financial Review* as one of its 100 Women of Influence. Her career reel is incredibly impressive, and includes being Regional Counsel Asia Pacific for JP Morgan Investment Management; Chief Executive Officer for the GO Foundation, an Australian Indigenous organisation founded by Adam Goodes and Michael O'Loughlin; and host of the Women's Agenda podcast series 'The Leadership Lessons'.

She is currently on the Boards of the Australian Associated Press, the Royal Australian Institute of Architects and Northrop Engineers Consulting, and is on the Advisory Boards of Mentor Walks and Propel, an organisation that manages digital reputation. She also consults with a number of organisations such as the Criterion Institute, the Paul Ramsay Foundation and the Melbourne Indigenous Transition School.

She has worked in Australia, Asia and the US. She has worked in corporate and not-for-profit. And, it seems, she is incredibly successful at everything she turns her hand to. I was intrigued to know if success is what made work meaningful to her. I was also intrigued to know how meaningful work has changed for her over the course of her extensive career. I was delighted that she agreed to be interviewed for this book, and pleasingly surprised by her answers – I hope you find her story as interesting as I did.

A VERY STRONG ACHIEVEMENT DRIVE

When Shirley was at school, she always wanted to be a doctor. Her dad had been a doctor, she adored him and wanted to follow in his footsteps. In about year 11 or 12, when she understood the hours that had to be put in to go through medical school and beyond, she realised she didn't want to work that hard and decided against it. She put the idea of medicine to one side, and didn't really think too much about university. In fact, she didn't really think too much at that stage at all about what she wanted to do instead. She completed her HSC and put all her focus on a Rotary Youth Exchange Scholarship in Japan she had applied for. She went there, spent a year learning Japanese, not thinking much about what came next. Initially she had wanted to apply to go to Sweden but her dad convinced her that Japan might be more useful from a business perspective for her career, which turned out to be a great decision, both for the reasons he recommended and because she met her future husband as a result of this exchange programme! Shirley arrived in Japan not eating rice, not being able to use chopsticks and not speaking Japanese. She got out of her relatively sheltered life, explored Japan, and lived with people she didn't know.

Returning to Australia, the only course she could get into at university was an arts degree doing Japanese and psychology, which she did and loved. Following this, she undertook a Graduate Diploma of Arts in Government which she also loved. Ever driven by learning, she didn't want to stop, so she then began a Master's in Japanese, and a friend of hers, who was a lawyer, suggested she should think about law, which she transferred to. It's clear from her academics, as well as from her biography, that she has a very strong achievement drive. We'll keep an eye on these themes of achievement and learning. They'll play out more than once in Shirley's meaningful work journey.

Once there, she applied for a number of roles in Tokyo and was successful in receiving two offers. She chose the one with law firm Cleary Gottlieb. As their first legal hire for the US outside of New York or Washington, they wanted her to spend some time in the New York office and pass the New York bar exam. Having only recently arrived in Tokyo, Shirley went to New York where she spent what she describes as 'a bunch of glorious months by myself doing the New York bar'.

She then returned to Tokyo, working for Cleary Gottlieb there for over four years. Life in Asia, working within law, at this point, was like living in a bubble. For the first year she travelled all over Asia, initially thriving on the excitement of it all. She was doing well, and that sense of achievement was strong, creating meaning for her. But for someone who didn't want to go into medicine because she didn't 'want to work that hard', she certainly was doing long hours. During that period, she estimates she was regularly working over 100-hour weeks. She was married by this stage, and both she and her husband had very high-powered corporate roles. With no children yet, Shirley would often do very long days. She tells of quite regularly (as often as three times a week) doing 28-hour days, where she would go in at 10 am and work straight through to 1 or 2 pm the following day with no sleep, then go home, have a shower, three hours' sleep and come back and do it all again. She enjoyed certain aspects of the work, but she recognised it was coming at a cost, mostly to her personal life. She wasn't seeing her husband. They weren't able to commit to anything outside of work. She tells the story of a ballroom dancing class they had signed up to at her behest. Shirley was barely able to show up, so she didn't improve. Her husband on the other hand had to partner with the dance instructor for the entire course and got much better!

She was never at home. She recounted an argument they had one night over a spoon. They'd ordered takeaway, and she'd served herself with the spoon then thrown it in the sink. Her husband asked her why she hadn't passed the spoon for him to serve with, commenting it was selfish, to which she replied, 'mate, just get a spoon'. As these things can, when we are under pressure, it erupted from there. Shirley took this as a sign. She knew they couldn't sustain this lifestyle. Shirley, as is evident already, had always been a high achiever, but achievement alone was not enough to sustain meaningful work for her at this point; and certainly not at the cost of her marriage, so she made the decision to leave.

She knew JP Morgan as a client, and they knew she was looking for her next thing and offered her a role. She worked with them, becoming Regional General Counsel of their Investment Management and Funds Management arms, which she enjoyed – it gave her new corporate and investment experience and she loved learning a new area.

She was with them for four years. She only left because her mum became unwell. Initially Shirley took a sabbatical, but her mum was dying of cancer, and Shirley was spending a lot of time going back and forth between Japan and Australia. By this stage, Shirley had two children. As a family they started thinking about moving back to Australia. This is an insightful example of how the sociological factor can impact meaningful work. How and what we choose to do for work is influenced by so much more than our own individual drivers, abilities and identity.

Some time passed between the thinking of, and actuality of, moving. Having been told by her mother's doctors that she'd likely get 18 months with her, sadly Shirley's mother passed away the Sunday after Shirley arrived back in the country. Understandably, this somewhat sent Shirley into a tailspin. They had moved countries. They had bought a house in Sydney. Her husband was still working in Tokyo but commuting, every week, spending three days in Sydney and four days in Tokyo. Her daughter was about to start school and she had an 18-month-old toddler. Nothing was the same for Shirley as it had been six months ago. All the ways in which Shirley determined work to be successful and meaningful for herself had disappeared. Her mum dying, in her words, 'played with her head a bit', and she wasn't in the right frame of mind to think about looking for a new job in Sydney. So, she decided not to do anything, filling her 'busy drive' through volunteering and charity work.

Shirley, who until this point had found meaningful work through her achievement drive and her desire to learn, did nothing, workwise, for 10 years while the children were young. She was fortunate, from the sociological factor perspective, that she had the means to take the break.

Then a big societal factor came along and impacted her work choices. One that impacted many people around the world at this time. The GFC. Just prior to the global financial crisis in 2008 her husband had been running his own hedge fund, and that had to shut down. He joined another hedge fund just before the crisis hit in 2008 but that was also affected. He decided he wanted to take some time off and spend some time at home as well. For two years they were both at home with the children together, which was great fun. They are fortunate they had the means to do this. However, it was another silly argument with her husband that was the turning point to get back into meaningful work for Shirley.

AT THE BOTTOM AGAIN

In October 2011, Shirley found herself for the first time in nearly 10 years looking for work. She had zero confidence, having been at home all that time. Like a lot of people who have been out of the workforce for extended periods, she worried about how she would go about making an application appealing to a prospective employer. Disappointingly, a huge number of headhunters told Shirley to stop wasting her time. However, a mentor advised her to look for a story she could tell about her time off from traditional work. She realised she had actually done all these great things during the time with her children, she just needed to create a narrative to tie them together and allow an employer to see the value those experiences meant she would bring. Within three months she was offered a job with Westpac. Despite previously having been a General Counsel, she was starting again there at the bottom of the legal ladder. Still, it was a start.

She didn't stay at the bottom of that ladder for long. Shirley initially worked on their financial advice and private wealth business, then moved to the leadership team for the private wealth business and then into technology and operations, before moving into Treasury. Treasury was very well respected within Westpac, and as a result several of their outstanding lawyers worked within that area. Shirley really enjoyed working with, in her words, 'super smart people'. As we know, one aspect of meaningful work is relationships, and this ticked all of Shirley's relationship boxes. Unfortunately, not all of it was meaningful. The job design aspect – the actual work itself – wasn't making her heart sing. The first year of this role was incredibly process driven. Shirley is a strategic thinker who enjoys the advisory side of law; she wasn't suited to the detailed nature of the work.

There was also a societal aspect of meaningful work that came into play. Shirley was one of only a handful of female lawyers on the whole floor. This impacted some key experiences Shirley had in the workplace, some of which she found incredibly frustrating. Unable to structurally change this environment at a pace that suited her personal needs for meaningful work, Shirley started a two-year process to look for something else. Determined not to go backwards again, she was applying for General Counsel roles and kept coming in second.

In one particularly frustrating moment, she came in second to one of the men who had been a previous cause of frustration for her.

Shirley is one of the most determined, resilient and smart people I've had the pleasure of meeting. Instead of giving up or settling for something lesser at this point, she decided to take it as a sign that General Counsel wasn't the right thing for her. Rather, she gave herself a year to think proactively about her career but not actually apply for anything. Her goal was to just go and meet with people and have career conversations. All the people she had been at university with were, by this time, on Boards, and in senior positions, and in General Counsel roles. She started meeting with them all.

A LIGHT BULB MOMENT

She caught up with a woman she'd been introduced to. They had a two-hour breakfast, where they'd got nowhere impactful in the discussion about Shirley's career. Just as Shirley was leaving, the mentor asked Shirley directly, 'What is it you actually want to do?' and Shirley replied instinctively, 'I want to run a P&L' (profit and loss statement). This was a turning point for Shirley. The mentor, as a result, helped Shirley get onto the shortlist for a CEO role of a large NFP that had an Asia-Pacific reach. She didn't get the role, but it gave her confidence that she could interview for executive roles and talk about her skillset in a way that senior people would have confidence in.

After that, Shirley met another mentor who asked her to complete a Strengths Profile. When they discussed the results, the mentor was surprised that Shirley was still even considering General Counsel roles. In the mentor's mind Shirley was a natural CEO, based on the collection of strengths the profile showed. Between this meeting and Shirley realising she wanted to run a P&L, a light bulb moment happened for her. Suddenly she knew exactly what she wanted to do.

Shirley decided to focus on not-for-profits. She went through a very thorough, very rigorous process to be selected as the CEO of the GO Foundation, her first CEO job and one of her favourite roles in her career. Interestingly though, despite the fact that this role gave her significant meaningful work, she nearly pulled out of the process before she'd even got the job, due to personal circumstances.

Shirley went through five rounds of interviews to secure the role. At the third round, her immediate family suffered a significant tragedy, resulting in a death, two nights before the interview. Shirley rang the headhunter and explained that she couldn't come to the interview. The headhunter, while sympathetic, noted that they had organised four directors to come together, and it couldn't be rearranged. Shirley explained what had happened and that she wasn't emotionally capable of sitting in a room and interviewing. The headhunter told Shirley, 'I'm going to say something, which will sound incredibly callous – but it's down to two candidates, and they need to move quickly. If you don't turn up – they will just give it to the other candidate.'

Shirley went on to tell me that the headhunter had asked her in previous interviews a lot about her family and her background, to get a sense of her. The headhunter said to Shirley that while she didn't know the person who had passed away, she suspected from what Shirley had said about her family, they would still want Shirley to go to the interview. She went to the interview and got through it. In the lift afterwards, Shirley describes feeling like a cartoon character sliding down onto the floor, and having some unsuspecting man rescue her in the lobby after she collapsed with grief.

She got the role. Her first CEO gig. The GO Foundation's first Chief Executive.

She *loved* it. She also did a remarkable job. In addition to significantly increasing the income for the foundation she also oversaw improved social media engagement, impressive increases in the number of beneficiaries and many other important metrics, helping lift the profile of this important charity. She was learning, she was achieving, and she was making outstanding contributions to society. This role really was meaningful, in every way, for Shirley.

THE NEXT PHASE

As the profile of the GO Foundation was lifting, the Board increasingly felt the importance of an Indigenous organisation being led by an Indigenous CEO, something Shirley couldn't change about herself. In a move that was sad for Shirley personally, but important for the Foundation, it was agreed that after just over four years in the role, it was important to make way for an Indigenous person to lead the GO Foundation for its next phase.

Shirley thought deeply about going into another CEO role. She felt like she'd done her time in corporate with her legal career. She had truly loved the GO Foundation, but it had an emotional toll. She had often found herself personally helping students in certain situations, which she gladly did. She told me a story, one of many, of one homeless student she spent some significant personal time with, ensuring they had food and accommodation. It was rewarding but not without emotional cost. She thought about the other types of not-for-profits she might be able to work with, and for a variety of personal reasons they weren't quite meaningful to her. She knew she didn't want to work with beneficiaries any more. She also knew she didn't want to do mental health, suicide prevention, sick kids or similar areas. The other areas she was interested in weren't looking for CEOs at the time she was looking.

She decided instead to enter the next phase of her career, her current phase, as a director, speaker and mentor. I asked Shirley about the themes of meaningful work, the things that have made her most happy and most unhappy during her career, and listening to her story the answers are fascinating. She adopted a new guiding rule: say yes until there is a reason to say no. This rule has led to many different opportunities coming Shirley's way, including some unexpected things like the 'Leadership Lessons' podcast.

The times she has been most unhappy at work are almost always tied to unfairness in some way. Two of these are societal. One we touched on earlier, the issues she experienced being female in a very male-dominated environment. The other though is interesting. She reflected on the point at which she felt like she realised she was not doing the kind of law she wanted to be doing. She went into law to make a difference. There came a point in her corporate legal career where there was a celebration over a big legal case that her large organisation won against a class action of customers. There was nothing wrong with this. For most people on the team, at the time this was truly meaningful. But for Shirley it wasn't. It created a disconnect. It reminded her that she had wanted to get into law to help those less fortunate. That desire to help was partly what had made the role at the GO Foundation so meaningful.

Sometimes her sense of unfairness, though, can be tied to organisational factors. She told me of times of poor leadership. We see in the theory of meaningful work that leadership is one of the most crucial factors to a sense of meaningful work, and two of Shirley's most painful stories sit in this bucket. So painful, I can't share them in detail (that's lawyers for you!). But it's driven her to want to be a good leader, and through her drive for achievement and constant learning she often seeks feedback on how she can grow and develop her leadership skills. It's delightful to observe how deeply satisfied Shirley is in her current phase of work, as she shares those lessons of leadership through her Board positions and consultancy work.

PART III

HOW MEANINGFUL WORK IS SHAPING THE FUTURE OF WORK

CHAPTER 14

HOW A GLOBAL PANDEMIC SHAPED MEANINGFUL WORK FOR AUSTRALIA

THE BEAUMONT PEOPLE MEANINGFUL WORK INSIGHT REPORT PRE AND POST PANDEMIC

In December 2019, just before the world was hit by a global pandemic, we released the 'Meaningful Work Insights Report' which uncovered what meaningful work was for Australians. It made for fascinating reading. Based on our research there were some hunches we had that turned out to be true and some things that surprised us.

Remembering that there is no right or wrong, and that everyone's path to meaningful work is unique, what do you think were the top three factors for meaningful work? If you've been paying attention as you've read the book, you likely already know the answers.

When I ask this question to audiences, people often get number three and number two right. In December 2019, in third place was purpose. That is, 'work which makes a difference' was the third most popular factor for meaningful work. In good news for the Australian organisations that participated, 75 per cent of people agreed that the core purpose of their organisation was to make a difference and contribute to society. But our respondents still felt there was work to be done, with over 60 per cent saying their organisation had no visible corporate social responsibility programme or not being sure if one existed.

In second place ... yep, the one people most often guess, the one that HR people and leaders go to first, the one that people think fixes everything: culture. Eighty-seven per cent of people at the time emphasised the importance of being able to express themselves at work, with the research showing that interaction with others and collaboration are strong indicators for meaningful work. Further, 85 per cent of people felt motivated and energised by engaging and collaborating with others at work to achieve team goals.

But surprisingly, taking out the top position in a pre-pandemic world was leadership, or to be explicit, 'having the trust of your managers'. Eighty-three per cent agreed they performed best when given the space to shape their own role, and 94 per cent need leaders to clearly communicate what the organisations wanted to achieve so they know what they are working towards. More trust but with clear communication and direction, the very crux of what makes leadership challenging.

The bottom three factors of meaningful work were all, in my opinion, somewhat surprising. In 2019 the lowest ranking factor of meaningful work was reward (pay), with only 4 per cent of respondents ranking it as their most important factor, meaning that, for 96 per cent of our respondents, factors other than pay rated as more important in contributing to their overall happiness and meaning at work. The second lowest was complexity of work, followed by positive feedback.

I find these surprising because as a recruiter these are what I call the 'pull factors'. The factors that 'pull' people towards a new job. By this, I mean these are the reasons we most commonly hear for people wanting to find a new role. These are the reasons a jobseeker will say out loud that they are looking for work because it is less insensitive or less political to mention if the money is better elsewhere or you are looking for more complex work. There are important reasons a jobseeker may tailor their verbal responses slightly in this regard. It doesn't make for a good interview if they are seen as being derogatory about their current employer, for example. What it shows, however, is how important it is if you are seeking work to be very clear in your own mind about which factors of meaningful work are genuinely important for you, and how you can articulate those factors in a professional way. If during your jobseeking process you are only articulating the factors that are least important to you, your chance of ending up in a role that is meaningful to you is much diminished.

THE POST-PANDEMIC WORLD

If you are wondering how the pandemic changed the face of meaningful work, you are not alone. If you changed how you felt about meaningful work during this time, join the club. If you are a leader and you have struggled to understand what your employees want to make them happy, or to attract and retain talent during 2021–23, it's you and every other leader out there. In March 2023, Beaumont People released their 'Meaningful Work Insights Report' from the data of the nearly 4000 people who completed a Meaningful Work Profile Tool from the launch of the tool in March 2021 through to December 2022, during the pandemic. And boy, were the results intriguing.

Coming in at number one during this timeframe was safety – physical, mental and emotional.[34] Workplace safety is now non-negotiable. This factor jumped a whopping 10 per cent. In 2019 only 60 per cent of

---

34 The comparison of the top three and bottom three is not exact because the first report was built from the research survey designed to build and validate the tool and the second report built from the data taken from those who had taken the tool itself, so there is some differentiation in the questions asked.

people strongly agreed that it was essential and that they would leave an organisation if they did not feel safe, but during the pandemic this rose to 70 per cent. It's encouraging to see this figure increase. Hopefully we are moving to a future where more organisations provide workplaces that genuinely provide that base level of safety that everyone is entitled to.

The second most important factor of meaningful work (remember I use 'important' really to mean 'popular'; there is no right or wrong) is team collaboration. The desire for collaboration has increased as a result of the pandemic. For example, under the individual factor of meaningful work, 95 per cent of people agreed overall with the subset that 'contributing to and achieving team goals motivates me', with 63 per cent of those strongly agreeing. This is up 8 per cent on the overall number from 2019, a sizeable increase. My hunch is that being isolated at home, separated from your teammates, drove an increased desire to achieve more with your team. We saw on my own MWPT the importance of workplace relationships increased from 2022 to 2023. It seems these themes have played out on a much larger scale.

The third ranking factor though, and it's good to know that we stayed the course in one area, is purpose, still coming in at the number three spot. However, interestingly the strength of desire for it is growing, with a shift towards those who feel strongly about it.

There were two other big positive swings worth highlighting.

The first is that career development is now critical. In 2019 only 58 per cent of people agreed that career development was critical to their success at work, but this skyrocketed a massive 20 per cent to 78 per cent through the pandemic. While much was written during Covid about people rethinking their priorities, potentially abandoning their stressful careers and moving to the country for quieter lives, this suggests instead that a growing majority are seeking career opportunities with progression. So much for quiet quitting!

The second is that innovative and creative workplaces are still in demand. Culture was in the top three in 2019, and innovative and creative workplaces is one of the subsets that plays into culture. In 2019, 82 per cent of people strongly agreed they would thrive in an innovative and creative workplace, with this modestly jumping to 86 per cent in the 2023 report. Strength of opinion grew significantly, however, growing from 37 per cent in 2019 to 51 per cent in the 2023 report. Given many workplaces have struggled to entice people back into their offices from the safety and convenience of their homes, this data suggests workplaces that stimulate them may be one way to encourage that.

The bottom three is, as ever, telling too. Pay is still the lowest. Even in a time when we saw record numbers of people losing their jobs in Australia. Perhaps by the time people were taking the tool the economy had picked up again – remember the MWPT was launched in March 2021 so the worst of the job losses were behind us in Australia by then. Ranking 'work is mostly a way to earn money' as the least important factor of meaningful work came in with only 21 per cent of people ranking it highly and only 6 per cent strongly agreeing.

However, second and third from the bottom were a surprise. They were the expectation of support in achieving personal goals and values alignment respectively. In the 2023 report there was a 5 per cent drop in the number of people who would not work for an organisation that provides products or services that conflict with their ethics or values!

MORE LOCALISED NEEDS

Our results reveal that the pandemic shifted attitudes to meaningful work towards the need to feel safe, contributing to team goals, purpose, valuing people before profit and career pathways. Less emphasis was given to money as a contributor to meaningful work and the need for support in achieving personal goals. Interestingly also, less importance was attached to working for an organisation whose products or services align with a person's ethics or values. While this contradicts with the desire for purpose, perhaps the pandemic has also ushered in a dose of reality for people who feared losing their jobs.

In many ways it appears we have made a shift towards what directly impacts us. Our needs are more localised, for ourselves and our teams, with a focus on safety, connection and purpose. As much as the data provides valuable insight, it also opens up some questions as we continue to work through dynamic times with new influences impacting attitudes to meaningful work.

Will the changes to workplaces be here to stay?

Will we seek more defined career pathways?

Will we see a rise in employee activism?

How will AI impact on the jobs and expectations towards meaningful work?

And how does all this ring true for you personally? Has the pandemic shifted your views? Have you reassessed what is meaningful for you? Has reading this made you reflect on what is important in your workplace as a worker, manager or leader?

CHAPTER 15

WORK/LIFE ... WHAT?!

THE GROWING DESIRE FOR INCREASED FLEXIBILITY

The most common question I am asked in relation to meaningful work, post pandemic, is, 'How much has the desire for flexibility increased as an indicator of meaningful work as a result of Covid?' You'll notice however that it didn't come up in the previous chapter. I'll come to why shortly.

It is a reasonable question. Vast swathes of us suddenly found ourselves working from home. And mostly we proved we could do it well (although Elon Musk seemed to want to argue otherwise!).

Stanford University released data in 2015 showing that remote working could be up to 13 per cent more productive.[35] This was showing up in the evidence coming out through the pandemic too. According to the Future Forum report, those who had full flexibility in their roles had 29 per cent higher productivity and 53 per cent greater ability to focus than those with no ability to shift their schedule.[36]

---

35 'The bright future of working from home', Nicholas Bloom, May 2020, Institute for Economic Policy Research, Stanford University. https://siepr.stanford.edu/publications/essay/bright-future-working-home
36 'Future Forum Pulse Executives feel the strain of leading in the new normal by a consortium of founding partners including slack', LT, MillerKnoll and BCG. www.futureforum.com/research/pulse-report-fall-2022-executives-feel-strain-leading-in-new-normal/

They also reported that remote and hybrid workers were more likely to feel connected to their direct manager and their company's values, and flexible remote work policies were cited as the number one factor that had improved company culture between 2020 and 2022.

While there are many jobs that simply couldn't or didn't lend themselves to working from home, those of us that were able to, did. Many of us found ourselves in that position for the first time. Some of us didn't like it. Some of us loved it. Some of us (me!) grew to enjoy it and over time relished the benefits of it. There was lots of speculation about whether it would change office space forever. Those discussions are still ongoing. How many days should we be back in the office? What is the right balance of connection, culture and collaboration? How do we balance deep work with connected work? How do we build relationships while simultaneously boosting productivity? As concerns around economic indicators rise, how do we create high performance and protect mental health?

Further, as leaders, how do we know if someone is performing if we can't see what they are doing?

The same Future Forum report had executives with 20 per cent worse work/life balance and 40 per cent more work-related stress and anxiety. How do we get this right for everyone across the organisation, and what do the meaningful work indicators tell us about this in our research?

So, to answer the question, 'how much did flexibility change as a factor of meaningful work as a result of the pandemic?', the honest truth is I can't tell you. And here's why. If you look at the detail of our academic research, you'll see that what we set out to do was to truly understand what makes work meaningful.[37] Which meant we needed

---

37 'Meaningful work and the development of a Meaningful Work Profiling Tool', Dr Jill Rathborne and Dr Elizabeth Shoesmith. November 2019.

to validate the various factors of meaningful work. Feel free to dig into it yourself so you can see exactly how, where and why, but to save you the hassle, the key thing you are looking for is the fact that the statement, 'hours that allow for free time and rest', didn't make the cut for validation and was deleted as part of building the Meaningful Work Profile Tool.

'But how can that possibly be?', I can hear you screaming at the book now. Well, here I am lifting this rock for you to look under and see for yourself, because if I am true to helping everyone find meaningful work, and if I am true to doing that in a way that stands the test of scrutiny, I need to be able to ensure that it is both validated academically and also explainable to the everyday person reading this.

The tool was built by developing statements after completing an academic review on meaningful work, which included flexibility. The tool then underwent a statistical validity process through model set up, data review and assumption checks, model reliability and validity determination, model fitting and iterative adjustments, and checked against demographic subsets. My understanding of this is that it is all academic speak for saying that some of the sentences had to be removed if they couldn't absolutely prove that there was enough evidence across enough people at the specific time of testing that the statement was a factor of meaningful work.

Our plan is to review all the academic literature and then retest the statement in due course, updating the Meaningful Work Profile Tool as needed, because we have proven that meaningful work changes over time. As such, it's likely that some statements will move in and some might move out, as societal factors play a part in shaping how we view meaningful work, so that the tool keeps up to date with evolving meaningful work literature and social norms.

Meanwhile, understanding the theory does mean you can still think about it.

DON'T WE ALL WANT A FOUR-DAY WORK WEEK NOW?

There has also been a lot of noise both in Australia and overseas about the rise of the four-day work week, and this is definitely something to consider when thinking about meaningful work for the future.

I'd be surprised if you haven't heard about the four-day work week but in case you have been living in a cave, or if as a leader you've been living in denial, let me give you the background.[38] It was pioneered by Andrew Barnes of Perpetual Guardian, New Zealand's largest corporate trustee company. It's a very simple concept. Staff who are employed full time on a five-day contract continue to get paid for five days but instead work four. Barnes started it as a trial in 2018 because he believed that he would raise workplace productivity as well as improve the mental health and wellbeing of his team. He made international headlines, won awards, and it was an undeniable hit. Now Barnes, along with his partner Charlotte Lockhart, are the founders of 4 Day Week Global. They are conducting trials across the United Kingdom, the United States, Canada, South Africa, Ireland, Australia and New Zealand, with more than 250 companies participating.

The UK trial was a resounding success.[39] Of the 61 companies that participated, 56 of them are continuing with the four-day week; that's a 92 per cent success rate. The key benefits were for the individuals. Thirty-nine per cent were less stressed and 71 per cent had reduced levels of burnout than before the four-day week trial. Also, levels of anxiety, fatigue and sleep issues all went down, while mental and physical health both improved. Work/life balance improved for individuals across the trial period. Fifty-four per cent said it was easier to balance work with household jobs, and they were more satisfied

---

38   www.4dayweek.com
39   'The results are in: The UK's four-day week pilot', Kyle Lewis, Will Strange, Jack Kellam and Lukas Kikuchi. Autonomy. February 2023.

with their household finances, relationships and how their time was being managed.

It wasn't just good for the workers though. Company revenue stayed broadly the same, rising by 1.4 per cent on average when weighted by company size across organisations. When compared to a similar period from previous years it actually increased on average by 35 per cent, which indicates growth even during a time of working hours reduction. And during a time of talent shortage, critically, the number of staff leaving the participating companies fell by 57 per cent over the trial period.

The final statistic that ties in with our results from the pre and post pandemic report in the previous chapter is how little impact money has for the participants. After joining the trial, 15 per cent of them said no amount of money would induce them to go back to a full-time five-day-a-week schedule having now become accustomed to the four-day week!

CHAPTER 16
THE FUTURE OF WORK

In late 2022, I spoke at the annual Clubs NSW conference on the importance of managing your workforce, a topic I often get asked to present on. In fact, the theme of attracting, retaining and developing people is a key theme that will repeat through the coming decades in any top 10 list of business challenges. It came in at number one of KPMGs 2023 list for Australian business, with 77 per cent listing talent acquisition, retention and re/upskilling staff to meet a more digitised future as their number one challenge for 2023, and 61 per cent ranking it their number one challenge for the next three to five years.[40]

WILL AI 'TAKE ALL THE JOBS'?

Despite the fear that artificial intelligence is coming and will 'take all the jobs', there will still be an ongoing need for human skills. But let's address artificial intelligence (AI) first. In 'Why "the future of AI is the future of work"', authors David Autor, David A. Mindell and Elisabeth B. Reynolds explain that artificial intelligence is far from

---

40 'Keeping us up at night: The big issues facing business leaders in 2023'. Alison Kitchen and Dr Bendan Rynne. KPMG. January 2023.

replacing humans, but it is significantly changing most occupations.[41] They point out that most of what AI can do, at the time of their book's publication (*The Work of the Future: Building better jobs in an age of intelligent machines*), is improve productivity and efficiency by using systems to look at vast amounts of data very quickly. There is still no AI that excels in 'social interaction, unpredictable physical skills, common sense and, of course, general intelligence'.

The big one at the time of writing is ChatGPT and the others coming like it. Have you tried it? Has your organisation?

Have people in our team used it to write job ads? Yes. So, is it going to impact their jobs? Yes. But there is no-one in Beaumont People whose sole job is to sit and write job ads. And ChatGPT will make our ad writing more efficient, but for some, the ads won't sound personal enough. The consultants will pick and choose depending on the role. What it will do is make them more productive, which will free them up to build more relationships, which is the bit that really matters.

Everything I've read on AI has me thinking that it will replace anything task based, anything that is repetitive or that requires vast amounts of data processing. Even ASIC are apparently using AI to assess reports, so it is certainly not only low-level roles that are at risk as the job landscape changes.[42] Essentially, if you think a computer can do it, it likely will.

Could that change over time as AI becomes more sophisticated? Maybe, but until and unless technology really does replace the art of being human, the human skills are the ones that matter. Let's turn to that now.

---

41   'Why "the future of AI is the future of work"', David Autor, David A. Mindell, Elisabeth B. Reynolds, MIT Management School, https://mitsloan.mit.edu/ideas-made-to-matter/why-future-ai-future-work. 31 January 2022.
42   'Gone in 38 Seconds: Regulator using AI to reject serious criminal complaints', Nick Bonyhady and Sarah Danckert. *Sydney Morning Herald*, www.smh.com.au/business/companies/gone-in-38-seconds-regulator-using-ai-to-reject-serious-criminal-complaints-20230303-p5cp7d.html. 6 March 2023.

According to the NSW Government's report, the rather nattily named 'Future Frontiers Analytical Report: Key skills for the 21st century: An evidence-based review'[43], the skills that will be needed in the future, as we move into a more digitised workforce, will be increasingly human and include:

- critical thinking
- creativity
- metacognition
- problem-solving
- collaboration
- motivation
- self-efficacy
- conscientiousness
- grit or perseverance.

THE HUMAN SKILLS OF THE FUTURE

Deloitte tells us that two-thirds of all jobs will be soft-skills intensive by 2030.[44] At the time of writing, unemployment remains at historically low levels. A quick Google search of 'talent shortage Australia' will find you any number of headlines predicting the shortage will go on for some time. Demographer Simon Kuestenmacher[45] believes that due to lower migration through the pandemic, by 2030, one million fewer people than expected will call Australia home, causing significant additional pressures on the talent shortages here. A Korn Ferry report has put the global price tag of this talent shortage at US$8.5 trillion in unrealised revenue.[46] As they wryly commented, we

---

43 www.education.nsw.gov.au/content/dam/main-education/teaching-and-learning/education-for-a-changing-world/media/documents/Key-Skills-for-the-21st-Century-Executive-Summary.pdf
44 www2.deloitte.com/au/en/pages/economics/articles/soft-skills-business-success.html
45 www.simonkuestenmacher.com
46 'Future of work: The global talent crunch'. Yannick Binvel, Michael Franzino, Jean-Marc Laouchez, Werner Penk, Korn Ferry. Spring 2018.

need to let go of the fear that robots are going to take over all our jobs and do more about the fact that we don't have enough humans to take on the human skills needed for the 85 million people they predict we will be short of by 2030.

So, we know the future of work is human skills, and we know there will be a shortage. What does all that have to do with meaningful work though? Here's an interesting observation: a number of those human skills are improved when you are engaged in meaningful work. For example, creativity is a skill you need. We have shown in our research that those who have meaningful work are more engaged, and further that more engaged employees say their job brings out their most creative ideas (59 per cent more[47]).

This is also true of collaboration. If you want people with collaboration as a skill you also need to provide an environment where it is safe to collaborate. According to Google's Project Aristotle, the number one factor in team performance is psychological safety, and if that isn't in place it doesn't matter how good an individual's collaboration skills are, they won't be able to collaborate with others.[48] Remember that our pandemic research showed physical, mental and emotional safety was the number one factor of meaningful work. The site teambuilding.com says Australia is third only to the US and Singapore in spend per capita on investing in its virtual team-building capabilities. Leaders have to create an environment where the human skills can flourish, as well as look for those who have the capabilities of those skills within themselves. These human skills of the future are part skillset, part environment, and are significantly enhanced by creating a meaningful work environment.

---

47 Krueger & Kilham, *Gallup Management Journal*, April 2007.
48 www.rework.withgoogle.com/print/guides/5721312655835136/

THE GROWING IMPORTANCE OF MEANINGFUL WORK

As the demographics of the workforce change over the next five to seven years, the face of meaningful work will also change. Boomers will leave the workforce (four million of them in Australia), and, as that happens, our Gen X population will increasingly take leadership roles (yes, that's me if you're interested). Simon Kuestenmacher predicts that with this they bring their values of work/life balance and gender equality, and that we will increasingly see these qualities significantly improve in workplaces across Australia. He predicts this will help reduce the gender pay gap at a much faster rate than we have seen previously. Let's face it, it couldn't change at a much slower rate, could it?! We know that flexibility didn't meet the validity criteria for the Meaningful Work Profile Tool in 2019 but had come up in the initial academic review, and the rise of the four-day work week seems to be improving outcomes for individuals the same way other meaningful work measures are, so an increase in this area can only be good for increasing meaningful work for the future.

In even more exciting news for the future of meaningful work, Kuestenmacher predicts that our young workers, our generation Y, 'obsess about meaning which leads to work image issues' in the way that previous generations have obsessed about body image issues.[49] Kuestenmacher worries this may lead to mental health issues; I see it as exciting, due to the opportunities it opens up. This is the very generation that will be filling the bulk of the gaps of those talent shortages. These are the people we need to help develop those soft skills. They are the people who are the future of meaningful work. Fortunately for all of us, they're already onto it. As ever, the young have realised it before most of the rest of us have caught on.

* * *

---

[49] www.thenewdaily.com.au/opinion/2022/07/30/the-stats-guy-young-workers/

If you are a leader and you want to give yourself the best opportunity to attract, retain and develop good people in what will continue to be a very tight talent market (notwithstanding usual economic cycles), developing an organisation that provides meaningful work across all four factors is the best way you can set yourself up for success.

And for yourself, of course you want meaningful work – I mean, who doesn't? But in terms of the future and what that means, let's think of it this way. That list of 'human skills' above – those skills are invaluable. No matter what job you do. No matter how good you are at them right now. No matter your age. If you are a teenager about to embark on your first job. If you are near to retiring. If you've been out of the workforce for some time. If you're a hotshot who's pretty bloody good at it all already. Who couldn't do with looking at that list and thinking about how they could improve at one, two or all of them?

CHAPTER 17
MEANINGFUL WORK PERSONAL QUEST: *Hamish Young*

Hamish Young is the Chief of UNICEF's Polio Eradication Team in Pakistan, a role he has had since July 2020. It is part of the Pakistan Polio Eradication Initiative, led by the Government of Pakistan and supported by the Global Polio Eradication Initiative. Prior to this, Hamish served in various positions in UNICEF headquarters, including as Deputy Director of Internal Audit and Investigation, and Chief of Development and Emergency Integration. He has also been the UNICEF Representative to Papua New Guinea, and the Deputy Representative in Tanzania, and the Eastern and Southern Africa Regional Advisor on Child Protection. He started his career with UNICEF as the advisor on humanitarian principles in Operation Lifeline Sudan. He has over 25 years' experience in leadership, strategic and emergency management, international human rights and humanitarian law, humanitarian relief and development work in Africa, Asia, the Pacific and the Middle East. He's had a very impressive and exciting career, and you may therefore assume is a bit of a coup for a book about meaningful work. But what makes his story truly compelling is how he got there. Because, you see, Hamish failed high school, scoring in the bottom 5 per cent of his year.

Hamish grew up in the North Shore of Sydney. For those of you unfamiliar with this location, it is a very well-to-do part of the country, with streets lined with large houses, with nice cars in the driveways and views to the harbour and ocean. Hamish enjoyed all the activities that went with growing up in this area, predominantly sailing and surfing, but he didn't come from a family that had as much money as a lot of his peers did. He grew up with what he describes as 'a very strong Protestant work ethic, despite my parents being nominally Catholic'. We're going to spend a little time on these societal factors that have influenced Hamish because we'll see, as his story plays out, how significantly they have impacted his career.

Hamish describes both his parents as borderline workaholic. Let's first look at his father. Dad, he tells me, was all lined up to join the army in the 1950s in the UK, before he emigrated to Australia. Unfortunately, Hamish's father was involved in a shooting accident and lost an eye, just before he was due to start at The Royal Military Academy. In those days there were no disability provisions, so he had no other pathway into a military career. Hamish's dad instead ended up having a mid-level marketing career, in which Hamish feels he was likely bored much of the time. However, he made up for it by getting his intellectual stimulation and contribution to society by involving himself in local politics. He ran a number of campaigns for local politicians, and then eventually ran himself and got elected. Hamish always had respect for the community service that was involved in his dad's political career. His dad continued with community service into retirement, working as a part-time volunteer for Meals on Wheels.

Hamish's mother had a significant career which also contributed greatly to society. She was a teacher. After this, she worked in TAFE, part of Australia's tertiary college system, and then moved into policy and administrative roles. She found herself working in human resources and other policy-based positions. Hamish spoke with such admiration of the focus his mother's work had during the 1970s and 1980s, where TAFE was providing a safe space and positive working environment for young migrant women from Eastern Europe and the Middle East who were discriminated against.

He told a story of the time when she saw some male family members of some of these young women, who didn't feel comfortable about their young female family members studying at a co-educational college. They would come to the TAFE and drive around at lunchtime to make sure none of the male students were talking to their daughters, sisters and nieces. She had a number of books published based on the work she was doing. She helped to shape the protection of these women and also influenced their levels of empowerment.

Hamish's early influence from his parents very much gave him a strong work ethic and a significant desire to contribute to society.

There were two other aspects that contributed greatly to Hamish's meaning in work. These were from the individual factors of meaningful work; the first was money, and the second motivation. He wanted to earn, and he was good at it. As a teenager, some of his peers' parents bought them things like trailbikes and sailboats. However, his parents always insisted that he earn at least half the cost of big-ticket items like these (and they usually provided the other half as a Christmas or birthday present).

Work was always motivating. Hamish says he was always quite average at most things during school, but he excelled at work. He was an average sportsman. He played rugby and enjoyed it but was average. He was average in track and field competition. He always struggled academically. However, work was something that always made him feel good.

He got his first 'job' at seven. He would earn 20¢ a day taking the trash out for two elderly women who ran the florist at the local mall. He'd stop by on his way home from school. The ladies weren't strong enough to lug the bag down the stairs into the carpark, so he'd take it down, throw it in the dumpster and be on his way. He'd earn a dollar a week for doing that and it doubled his pocket money. It was hugely important to him, and he continued to do part-time work through school. It made him proud that he'd finish the day being good at something even if he'd had a bad day at school.

Hamish failed his High School Certificate (HSC), so after school he took an enforced 'gap year'. He was able to quickly secure a warehouse job based on his sailing experience and work ethic with Whitworth Nautical World (as it was known then, now known as Whitworth Marine and Leisure). It was a ship chandlery and boating company. People would send in their mail orders and Hamish would send the items out. As Hamish had been sailing all his life, it was the best job he could have found. For a short period of time, it suited him perfectly.

Hamish loved sailing, and the organisation was great. But the job itself wasn't right. Hamish quickly became bored on a day-to-day level. After a couple of months in this job, Hamish thought about what the next 20 or 30 years of work might look like without any professional or even tertiary qualifications. It looked bleak, boring and unfulfilling. Hamish resolved that he had better go back to TAFE to re-take his HSC, and then go on and study a discipline that would allow him to do something more interesting than spending years and years packing boxes for mail orders.

A VERY DIFFERENT EXPERIENCE

Undertaking his High School Certificate at TAFE was a very different experience. This method takes a two-year high school curriculum and condenses it into an intense one-year full-time period with very little time off. Hamish explained that he essentially took a year 'off from life' and did little but study. He even moved in with his grandmother for the year. It suited his personality much better than school because it was all on him. The teachers didn't mollycoddle him; they didn't give him feedback or praise. He turned up or not, did the work or not. It's great for self-motivated students, and much more like the work environments Hamish had excelled in. He finished in the top 10 per cent of the state and was accepted into Macquarie University to study law and economics, where he went through the usual ups and downs but ended up finishing top of his year in law. Self-motivation is a strong driving force for Hamish and being left to his own devices seems to work for him!

From university Hamish took the traditional path of a law graduate into one of the large law firms and joined Mallesons Stephen Jaques. For a while, he loved it. He was a young hot shot, in a suit, running around the city. He was full of himself, going to court during the day and spending too much time at clubs during the night. He was living the life of a stereotypical corporate lawyer of the time. Like several lawyers he knew, his plan was always to do this only for a couple of years and then switch to becoming a barrister. As he describes it, he wanted to be doing the good-guy stuff and work on human rights, civil liberties and criminal defense.

He worked as a junior solicitor in the commercial insolvency and litigation team, and mostly they were responsible for bankrupting people and winding up companies. Hamish found the work financially rewarding and intellectually stimulating. Meaningful in those two aspects. But there were two things that weren't sitting well with him. The first was a gnawing feeling he had that perhaps he wasn't doing as well as he should on the detailed process side of the legal cases. Hamish, as you've probably gathered, has a large, strategic mind. He is quite obviously motivated by big, exciting projects and sometimes by stark deadlines too. But the minutiae and technicalities of some of the processes were not his thing. He was not confident he was doing his best in this regard.

The other was more existential, more a clash of values with his individual factors and his societal factors. He loved the intellectual stimulation and, in his words, the 'obscene amounts of money' he was making – well, they seemed obscene for someone who had just spent the last six years packing shelves at supermarkets to get through university. But he was increasingly feeling unsatisfied with what he was doing and how it was impacting others.

He told me a story about one day when he turned up to the registrar for a mortgage foreclosure hearing. Normally, there wouldn't be anyone from the other side, and it was simply a process thing you manage as a junior lawyer, and it was relatively easy not to think too much about the people involved. On this one occasion, however, a mother turned up with her little kids in tow. Her husband had left her after bankrupting the family, and she told the magistrate her story. It was the classic case of small business failure. The husband had been good at his job, but it turns out, as it so often does, that he wasn't so good with business plans, cash forecasting, stock control and all the rest of it. He took out a second mortgage on the house without telling his wife, and then as things continued to go from bad to worse, turned to drink to drown his sorrows before finally leaving her. Before she knew it, he had left her with two kids and a double mortgage that she previously had no idea about. And as Hamish puts it, here he was, the 'young prick in the fancy suit foreclosing on her'. These days there are laws in place to provide some protection in such cases, but this was all too common 30 years or so ago.

A LIFE-CHANGING OPPORTUNITY

These things were eating away at him, but he admits it may still not have been quite enough to leave a corporate legal career but for another life-changing opportunity that came his way. He had an old family friend who had a yacht and was sailing around the world, who was looking for some crew to help out. He had always dreamed of sailing around the world, and the friend approached him when he had only been with Mallesons Stephen Jaques for 18 months.

Hamish wanted to ensure he had at least two years on his resumé for consistency, so he didn't say yes immediately. While he was trying to decide what to do, most people thought he was crazy considering giving up a corporate legal career to go sailing around the world. However, he remembers one of the senior partners in the firm saying to him: 'You know, if you stay here, you might stay with us, or you might join another firm in time. And in 20 years you'll be very well off. You'll have all the trappings, including your own lovely boat. But, one night you'll wake up in your nice house, in a cold sweat, and you'll be mortified by the fact you had a chance to go sailing around the world and you didn't take it.'

So, Hamish took off and followed his dream, rather than following what might have seemed the most logical career path.

Hamish spent about nine months sailing with the family friend, and then went to work on some other boats. He was thoroughly enjoying himself. He was offered a job on a larger boat longer term and toyed with staying in that world for a year or longer. He was even considering whether he'd make a career out of it for a time, starting as a deckhand, making his way up through a charter company or similar, but reflected that the seven years he'd spent studying economics and law may be wasted. Ultimately, he ran out of money in Monte Carlo and decided it was time to make his way back to a corporate career. He hitched back to Calais, and he used his finely tuned negotiation skills to sweet-talk his way onto the ferry for a free ride back to London.

In London he went straight back into the big corporate law scene he had left in Australia, working with the biggest firm in the world at the time, Baker Mackenzie, doing exactly the same kind of work, living exactly the same kind of life. He was living in Covent Garden and making lots of money. This was an aspect of this work he loved. The theory of meaningful work shows us that everyone's path is unique, and that psychological factors and societal factors can sometimes be in conflict. We touched earlier on this, but I suspect that, for Hamish, having grown up in an area where his friends had access and means to certain things that he had to work for from a young age, it was deeply rewarding for him to have that kind of lifestyle, to be able to afford the kinds of things he couldn't when he was younger. Having enough money was, and still is, very important to him. Perhaps even more so now that he has a family. There is nothing wrong with that. As we have seen in the theory, there is no right or wrong, and everyone's path is unique. It is in fact one of the reasons why these kinds of career are deeply meaningful to lots of people.

The other aspect of this work that Hamish found himself in conflict with again was the detailed administrative part of the role. As in Australia, this is the area that Hamish didn't enjoy. Hamish admits he wasn't disciplined in the way he should have been around this side of the work. He also wasn't helping himself by partying hard. And then life helped him to make a choice. He was engaged by now but that broke down, and he got fired at the same time. In his words, it all went 'pear-shaped very quickly'.

AN INFLEXION POINT

This was an important inflexion point for Hamish. He had the luxury of time, having saved enough money to see him through while he worked out what he wanted to do. It was around 1993–94 and he was watching MTV at about 3 am, when a Bob Geldof concert came on. It dawned on him that it was an Australian crowd. Suddenly, he sees the beaming face of a disheveled woman in a black ball gown, and he recognises both the face and the dress, because it's the same woman in the same dress he'd taken to the North Sydney Boys High School Formal several years before; his old high school girlfriend. In what was known at the time as a 'drink and dial', he picked up the phone at 3 am London time, Sunday afternoon in Australia, and called her.

After chatting on the phone for a while, they found out they had both recently ended (or were ending) long-term relationships and in Hamish's words both needed to 'bail out' of their respective situations. So, six weeks later they met in Nairobi to travel around Africa. This is important because, as you'll see shortly, you could say that Hamish's entire career with UNICEF, and his happy marriage (still to come), is due to the fact that he was watching MTV at 3 am one night in London in the mid-1990s. A sliding doors moment.

Hamish and his friend backpacked their way around east and southern Africa for a while, having a great time and taking all sorts of risks and dangerous routes. His friend then headed back to Australia, needing to go back to work. Hamish had every intention of going back to Sydney to pick up his old plan of becoming a barrister. But he had found himself in some interesting situations in Africa, so instead he took a job in logistics with International Rescue Committee, an NGO. These are not-for-profit organisations that are independent from government organisations but usually receive some government funding and are established to aid social or political issues. While he found the overall mission and purpose very meaningful, the job he was doing was not fulfilling as it wasn't intellectually stimulating enough for him.

But, there were two significant events that happened. On the first day of his new job he met and fell instantly in love with Anna, who he would later marry and have a family with. The second thing that happened was that Hamish was transferred from the logistics support base in Kenya to Nasir, in southern Sudan, which was in an active war zone. Nasir was then invaded and overrun, and Hamish and his team were airlifted out and he was transferred to Rwanda.

Being transferred to Rwanda contributed to the changed course of Hamish's life. Arriving shortly after the genocide meant there were two big deployments of lawyers there. The European Union had a large group working on human rights issues, and the United Nations High Commission for Refugees also had a significant contingent there.

Hamish got talking to some of the lawyers and was inspired to see they had similar profiles to him. In his mind until that point, to be a human rights lawyer required a specialisation or some specific study, but many of these lawyers had very similar experience to him. In fact, he was somewhat surprised when he came across an old friend from his London office. They caught up for a few beers, and it turned out he'd been sacked too. As he said to Hamish, he wasn't surprised as his heart wasn't in corporate law, and he said, 'C'mon Hamish, you know your heart wasn't in it either.'

That's when Hamish started thinking that perhaps he could put these various parts of his life into the one role and career. He enjoyed the adventurous side of the work he was doing, in war zones in Africa. He didn't want to stay in administration and logistics, having invested seven years in an economics and law degree. Now he could see a potential professional pathway into development and aid via law. Kofi Annan had recently become the Head of the United Nations and he had set out a significant human rights agenda. Hamish recognised he didn't have the expertise in human rights law, but he knew there was a good legal library at the UN offices in Nairobi (remember, this is still in the days before the internet!). Hamish was still working with the International Rescue Committee, but he was spending as much time as he could in the library in Nairobi brushing up on his human rights and humanitarian law knowledge.

It paid off. He knew someone who was setting up a human rights and humanitarian principles programme as part of Operation Lifeline Sudan, who Hamish describes 'hassling' until eventually he was given a casual contract. It was just a couple of weeks, timed well as his NGO funding had finished. He was tasked with on-the-ground investigation of a massacre, and in his words, 'that was fascinating'.

This first short-term contract led to a couple more, which led to others, and then he was working for UNICEF. Under the United Nations interagency arrangements, at one point he was also working for the Office for the Coordination of Humanitarian Affairs. In this role he was the main contact for negotiating access with southern Sudanese rebel movements to get in and out of different places in southern Sudan. In some ways that's a radical shift from his corporate career back in Sydney and London, but as Hamish points out, in others it's really not all that different. He said: 'Negotiating with corporate bankers and negotiating with Sudanese rebels was 98 per cent the same skill set.'

THE BEST JOB HE EVER HAD

Hamish did this job for a couple of years and describes it as the best job he ever had. What made it meaningful to him was the coming together of some of the themes we've already seen: intellectual stimulation, and excitement, which suits his personal motivation, contribution to community, and a decent salary. But further, it was incredibly varied. One day he could be sitting under a tree in southern Sudan running a training programme for the rebel administration in humanitarian principles, and another he could be in Geneva for a high-level meeting hammering out a tripartite human rights agreement between the Government, the rebel movements and the United Nations. He felt like action man! Unfortunately, however, these kinds of jobs have a shelf life. Ultimately, people are rotated out of them and that was the case for Hamish.

He was by now firmly in the United Nations system, and his next position was a regional advisor working across east and southern Africa, training on humanitarian law with a particular focus on helping to demobilise child soldiers. It was an interesting role with lots of travel, which he did for three years. Hamish had married at the start of this assignment, and then after 18 months his first child was born. At that point all the travel, which had been a very positive aspect of the job, suddenly became a huge burden. So, Hamish then became the Deputy Representative for UNICEF in Tanzania. Having children changed the way Hamish thought about his career. He started thinking more broadly about how his decisions would affect them, factoring in more of the societal factors than he had considered previously.

He loved being in Tanzania, having been away from the ocean for so long. He enjoyed being able to sail again, loved the lifestyle. He was working on a range of child development and child rights issues, moving away from the legal side he'd known. It was fulfilling in some ways but not as intellectually stimulating in others, but it was ideal for the family, and this is what was starting to shape Hamish's career decisions. From a meaningful work perspective, as an outsider it's interesting to hear Hamish tell this part of his story. It sounds like this time of his life was in some ways much needed 'calm' but also somewhat a 'come down'. You get the impression he missed the adrenaline and the rush of his previous roles, but perhaps that was okay too.

From there he went on to be the UNICEF Representative in Papua New Guinea, where he enjoyed being the lead on the programme which gave him a little more freedom to pick the areas of focus he wanted to spend his time on, and he enjoyed working between child protection and some of the specialist legal areas.

He was lined up for his next rotation – most likely as a Representative in another larger country in the same region – but during their time in Papua New Guinea his son had been diagnosed with dyslexia and ADHD and it had been discussed with Hamish and his wife that his son would significantly benefit from some specialist schooling. Also, Hamish's wife became very ill in Papua New Guinea, with repeated bouts of vivax malaria and tuberculosis, among other things. Doctors strongly advised that she move somewhere with good medical facilities and no malaria. Family can be an important consideration in our careers. So instead of another Representative job in Asia Pacific, Hamish moved to New York, to take a role as the Deputy Director of Internal Audit and Investigation. Hamish talks of this role as being a really interesting mix of people. The audit team was full of auditors, the investigation team ex-cops, with there being an ex-FBI person in the team and some anti-terrorist squad people too, so it was a diverse and interesting group to lead.

For family reasons, Hamish stayed in New York as long as he could. He is grateful to UNICEF for the special dispensations it gave him to stay in New York for so long. The organisation factor has worked well for Hamish for many years now. He was still in New York at the beginning of the pandemic and enjoyed being at the forefront of the response.

The time came, though, for Hamish to move into another rotation, and he went to Pakistan to work on the Polio Eradication Programme. His three-year rotation there is coming to an end and he is now reflecting on what his next move within the United Nations might look like. His family is still in the US (his wife now also works for UNICEF in New York, and his kids are at college in Colorado and Connecticut), and he is understandably finding it tough not being with them. If he takes a family-friendly location, that means the family could move to be with him, which they are not ready for. If he doesn't and takes a more adventurous location it means living away from them but getting R&R breaks to fly back and see them regularly.

The theory of meaningful work has shown us that everyone's path is unique. Hamish has a unique blend of the individual factors of the need for intellectual stimulation, mixed with a personal drive for excitement and adrenaline. He has a strong societal factor of wanting to contribute to community, but also now that family piece around access is playing a part that is causing tension for him where it is in conflict with his individual factors. This has matched the theory in that we have seen meaningful work can change over time, as this is not something Hamish had to consider prior to having children.

I suspect we have caught Hamish in another sliding doors moment.

PART IV
WHAT NEXT? HOW TO DO SOMETHING USEFUL WITH THIS INFORMATION

CHAPTER 18

MEANINGFUL WORK PERSONAL QUEST: *Pamela Bishop*

Pamela Bishop is the Chief Operating Officer of Blooms The Chemist, an organisation she has worked with for nearly 17 years. She is also a member of the Australian Retailers Association's Sustainability Advisory Committee and The Marketing Academy's Reconciliation Action Plan Committee; a Director on the Board of Bambuddha Group; and an Advisory Board Member of the National Online Retail Association. She is a graduate of the Australian Institute of Company Directors and has an Executive MBA from the University of Wollongong. These are just two of the many qualifications she has achieved during her career. Yet she didn't go to college when she left school, and in fact her first job was in retail, in a pharmacy, and she has only ever worked for two organisations in her entire career, one in Ireland, and Blooms in Australia.

Pamela grew up in Ireland, and her parents worked in mental health and disability. They had a strong attitude around treating everyone with kindness and fairness, no matter their background, as well as a belief in the importance of community. This had an impact on her choices, in that she wanted to do something that helped others.

They also instilled in her a strong work ethic, while supporting her to make her own decisions around work. Pamela did well at school, but she didn't love it. She describes herself, at that point, as a very practical person who always had a drive to be productive. She had done some of the usual casual jobs while at school; babysitting, newspaper rounds, that kind of thing. Then, at the age of 15, she started working part time in the local pharmacy, Phelans. She had been accepted to do Social Studies at university, but it was in a different city, and she was young and had a local boyfriend at the time. So, she decided she didn't want to move away from home.

We'll see through the course of Pamela's story that the individual factors are always strong for her, and this is the first indication of that. Pamela knew what was important to her. She always had a passion for retail, and she had personal reasons to stay home. She made a decision in line with her own strengths, beliefs and goals, and she didn't move away to go to university. That decision shaped the course of her career. She stayed in Cork and went full time with Phelans instead, working with them for a total of six years, gaining much experience.

In 2006, when Pamela was 21, she decided it was time to do some travel and she came to Australia. Like a lot of people who come here, the initial plan was to come for a year, then travel round the world on the way home. But it didn't work out that way. She landed her first job in Australia within a week of arriving in Sydney. Her experience at Phelans stood her in good stead, and she was quick to secure a position as Retail Manager with Blooms The Chemist in Sydney's eastern suburbs, and sponsorship soon followed. Pamela stayed in this role for four years.

MANY DIFFERENT ROLES

What's interesting to note about Pamela's story is that, while she's only ever worked in two organisations, she's had many different roles within those organisations. After four years the first opportunity came to change roles within Blooms. She was approached to move into the corporate office in the business as their Merchandise Manager. The timing couldn't have been better. Pamela had initially loved her role as Retail Manager. She describes many of the aspects of working in pharmacies with such love and respect for what they do, the work with the community, the care for the health and wellbeing of the clientele, and Pamela's personal love for customer service and retail. But by this point she'd been doing the role for four years and was feeling the need to stretch herself more and learn something new. As a result, she jumped at the chance of the new job.

It was a significant shift for Pamela. It was the first time in her career she had ever been office based. She was used to being on her feet all day, not behind a computer. She was used to interacting with customers, not looking at a screen. She went from leading a team of 30 people in-store to being a team of just herself in the office. She was responsible for everything to do with the products, brands, pricing and supplier negotiations and she learnt an enormous amount during this time. What was interesting for Pamela, though, was that she had no experience in office-based culture, no understanding of what was normal or expected in this kind of environment, and was on a very steep learning curve in terms of the job itself. Her previously very strong individual factors, and her good job experience and job factors had stood her in good stead, and she assumed this would still be the case in this role, given it was the same organisation.

Here is a great example of where theory meets reality. It was the same organisation that Pamela had been working for in-store, but it felt like a different one. At the time, there was somewhat of a 'them and us' culture between corporate and retail, and even within the office there was some office politics that Pamela hadn't experienced before. Further, Pamela, looking back now, reflects that there was a lot of micromanagement, but being new to an office environment and new to the job entirely, she was unsure if this was just how things were done at the time. In addition, structurally, the way some of the practices were set up between corporate and the pharmacy outlets made it complicated for Pamela to do her job well, and she sometimes felt like she was trying to achieve things with one hand tied behind her back.

In Pamela's words, 'the job itself was really hard work for a number of reasons'. She says she learnt a lot during that time. She worked incredibly hard and did really long hours in those early days. She had no-one to show her the ropes, so she learnt by doing, often working 60- to 80-hour weeks. She actually thinks if you asked her at the time, she may have thought she was thriving because she was learning so much, and because she didn't know to think any differently about organisation culture. She knows that one of her individual factors is that need to feel productive, and she was definitely feeling very productive. There were also some great people she was working with.

But interestingly, looking back, she thinks of it now as a low point in her career. Her individual factors hadn't changed, but the job factors had. The organisation hadn't changed, but the organisational factors had, even within the same organisation due to the shift in culture, practices and processes. She wasn't feeling recognised and didn't feel her remuneration was in line with the contribution she was making. There were some people in the new environment she found herself in who were making the culture difficult to enjoy. She felt that the corporate environment at the time, especially in comparison to the retail environment she'd experienced prior, was very hierarchical and so she felt disempowered.

SUNDAY NIGHTS

There is a quote that Pamela loves, which is: 'Culture is how an employee feels on a Sunday night about going to work on a Monday morning.'

Pamela finally got to a point where this feeling on a Sunday night was not good, and she began to dread going into work on a Monday morning. She decided it was time to do something about it. She wrote up her CV, set up a LinkedIn profile and started looking at jobs on Seek. But the week after she had done all of these things, there was a change of CEO at Blooms, and Pamela decided to stick around and see if the change might impact things more broadly. This was 2013.

At first the new CEO seemed almost too good to be true. The first time Pamela met him, she recalls him saying various inspirational things, and she remembers him coming into the office on a Friday and asking if they had some wine and beers and cheese and crackers ready for the afternoon. They'd been so used to managing costs so carefully that it seemed too extravagant to them to be able to do that, and she said it meant so much to them. She remembers there were many little things over time that changed, and these little things added up to change the culture significantly.

Notably, when I asked Pamela to detail her happiest time at work, it is the time immediately during this phase with the new CEO. Pamela credits him with teaching her a lot about leadership, and specifically the difference between management and leadership. She quotes him as saying, 'Managers manage things, budgets, tasks, deadlines, but leaders lead and inspire people.'

Pamela states this is true of him, and it inspired her to want to start on her own leadership journey. It was also a time when her career was at a pivotal point. There were three specific aspects of meaningful work that came together at this time. She was heavily involved in the conferences their organisation participated in, both their own internal conference and attending others. As a result, she travelled all over the world visiting best-in-class retail pharmacies. She went to Las Vegas, Cape Town, China, London, New York, Paris and Hong Kong to name a few places.

She loved the travel – and the retail opportunities that came with it! The travel also broke up the time in the office. It was always full-on when working in the office and she missed the action of being on her feet that came with being in retail. The second aspect that was meaningful about the travel component of this role was it often gave her one-on-one time with the CEO, whom she admired and learnt so much from, while on the plane or walking around a shopping mall to review the pharmacies, for example. The learning opportunities this presented were second to none.

The third aspect of meaning that came out of this was that it opened her up, for the first time, to some social responsibility opportunities and more cause-related work. She told me about a project she was involved in when she was in Zambia, which she describes as the most rewarding experience of her career. Pamela was in Zambia with two colleagues, preparing for a conference they were having there later that year. They got to visit a health clinic in a very small hospital in a town called Simonga. Pamela describes it as having been shocking. Babies were being born in the same areas where patients with HIV were being treated, so there was a high risk of cross contamination. There was no running water, and a lack of facilities.

To get to the hospital to have their babies delivered in this environment, women were walking, while already in labour, up to 11 kilometres through the local African terrain. This included walking past whatever – sometimes dangerous – wildlife happened to be around at the time. Potential stampeding elephants was the biggest concern.

Pamela and her colleagues knew they had to do something about it. Using her characteristic persistence, they looked into what it would take and set about doing so. Blooms The Chemist funded the building of a maternity ward and women's shelter. It doubled the size of the hospital and moved new babies away from the HIV clinic. It also meant the pregnant mothers could come just before they were due, rather than when they were already in labour, given the women's shelter provided space for those who had further to travel. What an achievement for Pamela and her colleagues.

A SHIFT IN FOCUS

Pamela observes that over time meaningful work has shifted from a focus on herself to a focus on others. She feels this is reflected in her leadership mindset too. Ten years ago, she was very focused on her own personal development. She was doing a lot of studying. She undertook several courses to make her better at her job. She set herself KPIs and personal achievements she wanted to meet, and it was important to her that she always felt like she was kicking goals. Those individual factors were very much at play. They are still important to her, particularly the learning and development. She believes she will be a lifelong learner. The shift that has happened, though, is where that focus now lands for her. She thinks much more now about how she can help others reach their full potential. Meaningful work now is about how she can help someone else develop and grow.

The significant change that occurred for Pamela that influenced this was a societal factor. She became a mum.

Prior to this, Pamela had transitioned through a number of changes within her role and also a promotion. Under Blooms' new leadership, with a strong emphasis on culture, it was like working for an entirely new organisation and the team grew, creating new opportunities.

In 2016 Pamela became the General Manager for Merchandise and Marketing. She'd worked with the marketing team since moving into the corporate area but was now overseeing that team, so it was a really interesting time. She was having to focus a lot on culture and alignment as she brought the two areas of merchandise and marketing closer together.

They were implementing a lot of change which was challenging, and it taught Pamela a lot about change management strategies. She was involved at this point in an e-commerce project in China which she found interesting, and it was also during this period that she was doing a lot of her own professional development, so it wasn't unusual for Pamela to get up early, study from 4 till 6 am before doing a full day's work. She describes it as an intense but exciting period.

In 2019 Pamela had her first child, returning to work in early 2020 to the newly created role of Chief Marketing Officer (CMO). She was very excited about this role, but also had some trepidation, given that she isn't a qualified or trained marketeer. Her main focus was to operate at a more strategic level, and she asked herself two questions: where can I add value? And what can I put my stamp on?

Pamela knew that Blooms was already doing great work in the community, and she saw an opportunity to try to harness that for greater impact. She was increasingly understanding the importance of the social responsibility space and knew that they'd really only scratched the surface so far. She had been reading a lot about responsible business practice and saw a real opportunity to add value through ESG (environmental, social and governance).

Again, the timing worked out well. Just as Pamela had been given the opportunity for this newly created role of CMO, in which she had a lot of freedom to design it to make it meaningful, she'd also been accepted on to a personal development leadership programme for high-level marketers. It was a nine-month programme and through this she met a number of people in the corporate social responsibility space. This included the CEO of Bambuddha Group, who specialise in helping organisations to embed kindness into practices to underpin their ESG priorities. Pamela saw an opportunity in how these principles could apply within Blooms and the two started working together, doing, in her words, amazing things!

ANOTHER PAUSE

Pamela's career soon had another pause, with the birth of her twins, and in just over two years she found herself with three young children. We're at early 2022 by the time Pamela returned to work and again she found herself with a lot happening. In addition to the three little ones at home, there had been an office move to a new location. The CEO, who'd long been a mentor to her, had decided it was time to retire, and while he is still involved in Blooms as a Director on the Board, she came back to a new CEO, which naturally involves a lot of change in the business. This CEO promoted her to another newly created position on her return from maternity leave, this time to Chief Operating Officer (COO).

Pamela observes that one of the aspects of Blooms that she admires is that both times she has been on maternity leave she has come back to promotions, and that those conversations have happened with her while she has been on leave. She is aware that a lot of people still, unfortunately, experience their career taking a step backwards or stalling while on maternity leave, but the experience for her has been the opposite and she's immensely proud of Blooms for that. She's been in the role now for just over a year. She is also the chair of their internal ESG committee.

Let's jump back to how becoming a mum really changed her views on the societal aspects of meaningful work. Pamela describes becoming a parent as a life-changing experience. Her husband has always been incredibly proud of her career, and she describes him as her biggest supporter. They've managed the parenting well between them. However, she reflects on the level of responsibility that comes with it and feels the weight of that responsibility quite heavily. She's very aware a lot of bad things can happen in this world and worries about that for her children. She doesn't like to watch the news for example, describing it as 'too bloody traumatic half the time'.

In the last three years in particular, it has become clear to Pamela that she wants to spend her time doing something that will create an impact. It's important to her that she works for a company that takes their social responsibility seriously. She believes business has a role to play in making the world a better place for future generations. That is really important to her, yet it is not something she would have considered five years ago. While she knows it's important for individuals, she sees it as crucial for organisations too, because they have the resources and can be a force for good.

Pamela is incredibly proud to have led Blooms The Chemist Management Services to achieving B-Corp certification. B-Corps are businesses that meet high standards of social and environmental performance, accountability and transparency, and it is recognised across 85 countries. It takes a significant amount of work to achieve this certification and Pamela describes it as a challenging but rewarding experience. There is a lot that goes on behind the scenes to meet the requirements for this, and it is certainly another indication of Pamela's tenacity that she was able to overcome these hurdles.

Blooms has over 100 stores and over 2000 employees. It is not a small organisation. Implementing anything within an organisation that size takes a lot of hard work, change management, perseverance and dedication no matter your role or level of seniority. Pamela credits what she learnt about leadership mindset and change management through her career, combined with her absolute belief that it was the right thing to do and her tenacious personality, as the drive that kept her going. As a result, she, and the whole team at Blooms, rightly count it as one of their most notable achievements.

Pamela is at another interesting point in her career. She has been the COO for just over a year and, by the very nature of the role, it is more hands-on and less strategic than her previous job. She recognises that company purpose, ESG and social responsibility areas are the factors that are now most meaningful to her. Two of the job factors of meaningful work are job expectations and job design. Her individual, organisation and societal factors are very much being met. Pamela has learnt that she has a little to do to shape her role further, to ensure her role sits within her current expectations of meaningful work, while also meeting the needs of the organisation. She hasn't learnt this through theory but through her own personal experience of meaningful work. Fortunately, as we've seen, she works with a forward-thinking organisation who also believes in creating meaningful work for its employees, and she is currently enjoying productive conversations with her CEO on that very topic.

Blooms' websites talk about being passionate professionals committed to making a difference in communities all around Australia. Pamela's story demonstrates the truth behind this statement.

CHAPTER 19
WHAT'S NEXT FOR YOU?

How have you felt as you have read this book?

I'm sure you've had some great 'a-ha' moments.

Have you been scribbling furiously in the margins or highlighting with the e-reader as you've gone along? And making notes in your notebook?

Has reading this made you question whether you have meaningful work?

Has it made you have a complete career crisis?

Or have you more than once thought smugly that you are completely happy in your choice of job or career?

If you have read this far, chances are that it has got you thinking on some level, and that is great. In fact, it is fabulous. I'm excited that you're thinking about meaningful work! But I do want to sound a word of caution. The world of work is complex, and work is one part of our lives that intersects with the other parts of our lives in many ways. I have written this book to complement the great work we do at Beaumont People in connecting people to meaningful work and creating more opportunities for meaningful work.

Don't rush your next steps.

Too often we see people seeking new jobs making the same mistakes again and again and repeating the same patterns, not truly understanding what it is that is making them unhappy in their work. The information I have shared in this book, and the tool we have built, will give you the guidance you need to break some of those patterns. Use it wisely to think deeply and reflect for yourself on what makes work meaningful for you, remembering that it is unique, that it can change over time, that it is shaped by both sociological and psychological factors and that it includes individual, job, organisational and societal elements.

Here are the steps I suggest you take next:

1. Take the Individual MWPT and review your notes throughout this book.

Review your meaningful work profile (MWPT)[50] or perhaps take it again if you last did it a while ago (it's free – do it as many times as you like!). Remember, don't fall into the trap of saying you 'strongly agree' with *everything*. All the factors of meaningful work are nice to have, but, for example, do you really strongly agree to being energised by working with others? Or are there times when working with others is draining? Does it depend on who the others are? Or does it depend on how tired you are to begin with? Are there times when you need some quiet to regroup and regain your energy? Be really honest with yourself here, because this tool is only there to help you. The more honest you are, the more useful the tool will be in helping you find work that is meaningful for *you*.

Secondly, take a look at the notes you jotted down as you answered the questions and exercises throughout this book. If it helps, collate them so you have them in one document.

---

50   www.meaningfulwork.com.au

2. Take inspiration.

Remind yourself of our six personal journeys of meaningful work we shared to see if there were any stories that rang true for moments in your own career. Had they had times that reminded you of your own inflexion points? Were some of their challenges similar to yours? Can you take inspiration from any of the ways in which they have moved towards meaningful work when they have found themselves not aligned to their own factors of meaning?

3. Consult.

Find someone who can be objective – a friend or relative, coach or mentor you trust who is not emotional, who won't guilt you into feeling a certain way, who doesn't trigger certain feelings when you discuss certain topics, and now that you understand the sociological factors, isn't likely to influence you in that way against your own preferences. Someone who can call you out where you may lack self-awareness of your own weaknesses on occasion. Chat it over with them. Find time to do this properly. Book it in with them, over a coffee perhaps (your shout, I suggest …). Prepare them so they have some context. Better yet, get them to read the book, take the MWPT themselves, or both.

4. Act with clarity.

Through that consultation start to clarify your action points. Where in the factors of meaningful work are your pain points? Do they sit in individual, job, organisation or societal? The questions to discuss and resulting actions will be determined somewhat by the quadrant they sit in. As you discuss, understand and think about the push and pull factors. Push factors are those that make you want to leave a job, the things you currently don't like about something. Pull factors are those making you want to move towards something new, the factors attracting you towards a new job.

Just like dating, a new job isn't always better than the last one, so it's important to be really clear on what your meaningful work profile is before you take any action, so you can act with clarity. It may well be that you can stay in the role you have and dramatically improve where you are, without having to go through the effort of changing jobs. Sometimes a tweak in the way the role is designed so that you can work to your strengths can make a significant difference to how meaningful the work can be, and you might be surprised at how receptive your leader is to a conversation about creating meaningful work. After all, don't they also want to create workplaces that are more likely to overcome the number one challenge for organisations in the next decade?

CHAPTER 20
WHAT'S NEXT FOR BUSINESS LEADERS?

Solving the challenge of meaningful work will be the greatest leadership challenge of our generation. That's a bold claim, I know. But, as we've seen, the evidence is in. The talent shortage is our biggest business issue. Human skills are our biggest talent problem within that shortage. The data shows that generation Y – the dominant workforce group with an expected 42 per cent of the workforce by 2030 – are driven by meaningful work. If you want your organisation, your leadership, to succeed in the next five to 10 years, you need to become serious about this, now.

So what can you do? Well, start by getting serious about meaningful work for yourself. Hopefully you've read this far and have applied all the theory to yourself, because guess what? If you are in meaningful work, chances are you'll be much better at providing more meaningful work for others! Start with yourself is my first tip. Then it gets a bit more complex, and solving the organisational challenges of providing meaningful work is, and may well be in the future, a whole book in itself.

But let's look at some practical things you can apply today to start to move the dial in the right direction.

1. Observe.

All of the theory that's been shared with you in this book can be applied at an organisational level. You can reread sections and apply the questions with a lens of 'how well does my organisation do this?' You can observe how well your organisation performs in these various areas across the four factors of meaningful work and start to assess what you might like to improve. You could observe externally too. What are your competitors doing? What about other industries you could learn from?

2. Ask.

You can ask your colleagues for some input into the factors of meaningful work, then build it into your team meetings, into your one on ones, into your performance reviews. You could ask them in what ways you, as their leader, could provide more meaningful work, and in what ways the organisation or job could be more meaningful. You could then review what could be implemented to take that feedback on board. You could also ask externally; do you have trusted people within your industry whose opinion you could solicit, for example?

3. Survey.

You can use our Organisational MWPT tool to see how well you are officially going against the evidence-based measures of meaningful work and then consult with us to decide on which of the measures you want to work on and incrementally look to improve on those over time. You can track how your improvements are measuring and how your different departments compare, and see how these impact against all the factors of meaningful work.

4. Act.

Most importantly, but critically with clarity, you act. Not on gut, or on fear, but based on the trends that are predicted to make businesses succeed in the future, and in the areas that are proven to help organisations attract, retain and keep key talent in a world that is fast changing to a workforce that still requires human skills and where the future of work is meaningful work.

CHAPTER 21
CONCLUSION

Wow. That's a lot, right? How are you feeling? Excited? Energised? Exhausted? Overwhelmed? All of the above? If you cast your mind right back to the very beginning to the introduction, I mentioned that finding meaningful work was a bit of a Holy Grail. Now you know why. Like anything worthwhile it isn't necessarily easy. If it was, we'd all be happily skipping to work each day and leaving at the end of the day whistling all the way home.

Let's take a moment now to summarise what we've covered. Let's pull it all together in a way that will help you remember the key things you need going forward to ensure you can keep moving the dial in favour of meaningful work for yourself.

First let's remind ourselves of the definition of meaningful work:

Meaningful work is the importance an individual places on their work meeting their current personal beliefs, values, goals, expectations, and purpose in the context of their social and cultural environment.

This is important because it goes to the heart of our first key message of the book, which is:

1. **Everyone's path to meaningful work is unique.**

   It is crucial that if you take nothing else from this book, that you take this. Meaningful work means different things to different people, and that is okay. The personal stories showed us very different stories, very different people, each of them seeking different types of work and different ways to make their work meaningful. There were some similarities – for example, they all wanted to help people, although the expression of how they went about helping others was incredibly varied. Yet there were lots of differences too. For some of them money was more important than others. For some, career progression was more important. For some, leadership had greater impact. There was a lot of diversity when you dug into it. It is really important that *you* take the time to work out for *you*, based on *your* beliefs, values, goals and so on, what meaningful work is.

The second key message you need to remember is:

2. **There are four factors of meaningful work: individual, job, organisational and societal.**

   Knowing these, understanding what they mean and the subsets within them and how they interplay, is crucial to getting to the heart of meaningful work. It is what will allow you to understand how meaningful work is unique to you. All of these factors are proven to improve meaning in work, but you don't need to personally focus on every single one of them, only on those that matter to you. By measuring and monitoring these factors you can start to see how they are impacting you in your current role, or in your job search.

You may begin to see where there is tension between certain factors, as we have seen in Hamish's story. In his example in the individual factor, his personal motivations are aligned well with his job but are currently somewhat in tension with his societal factor in that they don't suit his family needs. This may have helped you to realise where you have tension. Or different examples may have helped you realise where you thought you had a challenge with the job factor, rather you have a challenge at the organisational level. Thinking deeply about these factors and how they influence your happiness, engagement and performance at work will help you assess what steps you can take to create more meaning.

Finally, don't underestimate how important the societal factor can be. Make sure you are aware of how big an impact it can, and does, have on your life, and be comfortable with the decisions you are taking because of it. If it is causing tension for you, find a way to make peace with that. These societal factors can be important – friends, family, faith, beliefs, values and the like. They're not easy to resolve if they go against our individual factors, but find a way through if you want to find your unique path to meaningful work.

Don't forget the third key message:

3. Meaningful work changes over time.

This was consistent through all of our examples. They have all had fascinating careers, and all at various times found their work meaningful and then not, depending on what was happening in their lives. Just as you find meaningful work, something might change and you might have to tweak, adjust or completely reassess what you are doing to reattain meaningful work. Knowing this though, you can stay one step ahead. Be aware of your factors, be aware of what might be changing for you, know that big life changes are likely to change what makes work meaningful. Be aware that changes to your job or organisation are likely to change what makes work meaningful too. Keep those things in mind and keep measuring it and staying on top of it. Like health, it's a habit that gets results rather than an outcome that is fixed.

THE FUTURE OF WORK IS MEANINGFUL WORK

It's important as you think about and reflect on what meaningful work means for you that you understand it in the context of the changes that have happened and are coming. Were the changes that occurred for the majority during the pandemic the same as you experienced? Further, let's not forget that work/life balance and flexibility are worth considering. It wasn't valid in 2019, but we know meaningful work is unique. Is it something that you need to consider? Did it change for you because of the pandemic? If so, think about how and why and what you can do with that information. You can't go past reading about the four-day week. Andrew Barnes and his team seem to me to always be looking for more organisations to participate in the trials!

Finally, think about your job and how it is likely to change in the context of the changing workforce. AI will impact every role in Australia, in our region and globally. Think about what human skills you have and how they will continue to be needed. Think about our examples and how their human skills were often the same regardless of where they were in their stories. Mimi's love of interaction and action orientation was the same when she was a volunteer tea-girl as now being the owner of a multi-site private speech pathology practice. Hamish's love of action and sense of adventure were the same skills that saw him sailing on boats as a deckhand and working as a negotiator for the United Nations in warzones. Shirley's love of learning and drive for achievement saw her take up a placement in an exchange scholarship programme in her youth and her first CEO role.

Todd's keenness on problem-solving and desire to leave a legacy were the same whether designing a right-hand turn or changing the future of an entire organisation. Matt's love of helping others, and not letting them down, was the same skill that let him enjoy working in a warehouse and running his own recruitment firm. And Pamela's strong sense of determination is the same skill that saw her stay at home and work in a pharmacy rather than take up a university place, and later saw her lead another pharmacy to achieve B-corp certification.

BECOME PART OF THE MEANINGFUL WORK GENERATION!

For this book to be truly life changing it's what you do next that counts.

I've said it before, and I'll say it again. Meaningful work is a Holy Grail. It is hard and it takes effort. It takes dedication and perseverance. It is one of the most rewarding things you can do. It will give you significance, meaning, purpose, independence, connection and joy.

I encourage you to take a look at the notes you wrote when you completed the exercises through the book and revisit your Meaningful Work Profile Tool one more time. Gain some real clarity on what meaningful work is for you, and what you want your next steps to be. Reread the personal stories and see what rings true, what inspires you or what sparks a thought for you.

Ensure you've understood the theory so you can be better placed to know when something has changed for you in the future around meaningful work. When you find yourself unhappy, you'll know to ask yourself at a high level first, 'is it individual, job, organisational or societal?' Then start breaking it down from there. You'll have a diagnostic to help you take some steps to see if you can resolve the situation.

Work out which bits matter to you more than others, and work on tweaking those dials. Don't chase perfection – it doesn't exist. We work with humans, who are imperfect. There is no such workplace that provides every factor of meaningful work. But work on the ones that are most important to *you*.

And then just keep doing it, every time something changes. Which doesn't necessarily mean changing jobs every time. It means adjusting, tweaking, discussing, changing, working to your strengths. It might be the very thing that keeps you in your job longer. You might be the person who helps make your workplace more meaningful. If you share some of these ideas with your team and your leaders, they might work on some of it with you. Together you might create more meaningful work for everyone. Then you will truly be creating meaningful work!

ACKNOWLEDGEMENTS

So many people to thank.

First, thank you to the love of my life, Paul Mapson. You have supported me in meaningful work for more than 20 years, and always encouraged me to achieve my dreams. We are a team, and I couldn't do what I do, achieve what I achieve, without you on my side, by my side, so thank you.

Thank you to my son, Callum, who so often kept me company while I wrote. Sometimes doing homework, sometimes gaming, but often there in the office alongside me. Also, thanks for brainstorming titles with me, and sorry 'Taming the Meaningful Work Monkey' didn't get up. Next time, buddy.

For the facilitation, inspiration and continued reflection on meaningful work, thank you to Carolyn Butler-Madden. Thank you also for allowing me to pick your brains on all things editing, publishing and book writing. Much appreciated.

To the brilliant people who agreed to be my case studies. I had an inkling, but no genuine idea how great your stories would be when I first approached you. Thank you for being so open and honest, and for being part of this process. I loved hearing about your journeys and am sure the readers will too. I really appreciate you being involved, Matthew Sampson, Hamish Young, Pamela Bishop, Shirley Chowdhary, Mimi Naylor and Todd Halliday.

For anyone who has enjoyed reading this book, significant credit needs to go to Michael Hanrahan and Anna Clemann at Publish Central. Thank you both for helping me with the editing, designing, advice, publishing and generally putting up with my endless emails and so much more. I have really valued working with you.

To Nikki Beaumont, who established the first company in which I found truly meaningful work across all four factors, and in which I now have the freedom to create meaningful work for others. Thank you for the opportunity, and for the great fun and success we enjoy in working together every day.

Two people within Beaumont People deserve special thanks by name. Rebecca Rynehart who heads up our consulting practice. Thank you for your contributions to the chapter on the individual factors of meaningful work. And to you and Sarah Ferraina, our Head of Marketing, I also want to thank both of you for your ongoing commitment to and belief in the value of meaningful work and getting the message out there. Sometimes it feels like the world is slow to come around to our way of thinking but I appreciate the time, effort and resources the two of you in particular have put into the Meaningful Work Profile Tool with me over the last couple of years. And, I'd like to thank Dr Liz Wilson and Dr Jill Rathborne for the initial research into meaningful work.

To the rest of the team at Beaumont, I can't think of better people to spend my working days with and love that we get to create so many meaningful moments together, so thanks to each and every one of you too.

I'd also like to thank Charles Cameron, CEO of the Recruitment, Consulting and Staffing Association of Australia and New Zealand. From our fortnightly catch ups over the last four years, through to the many projects, events, lobbying, working groups and other things we have worked on together, your passion for higher ideals and optimism to lead in the world of work have often been more inspiring than you know. Thank you.

Our Leadership Think Tank Group, a peer advisory board, led by Jason Tunbridge, of which I've been a member for over six years.

I'd like to thank you for the advice, mentorship, guidance and counsel. Thank you all: Anthony Elkerton, Alex Wilson, Andrew Simpson, Justin Wimpole, Sarah Hosking, Todd Halliday, Tean Kerr, Zoran Jusic, Laura Hamilton-O'Hara, Shirley Chowdhary, Elisha Renton, Brigitte Coldicott. You've all made me a better leader, businessperson, actual person.

To everyone at the NORTH Foundation, from those on the Development Committee with me, to the Board and the team themselves, thank you for allowing me another avenue for meaningful work. To be a small part of the amazing work you all do in connecting patient care and community wellbeing with world-class medical research truly creates meaning for me.

I'd like also to thank everyone who believes in meaningful work – don't give up on the quest. Keep at it; like anything worthwhile it takes effort, but it is worth it. The more of us that do it, the more we will generate it, the more meaningful work we will create.

And two final thank yous.

To my close friend, TK Peupion, who I walk with every Saturday. Her day-to-day world is so very different from mine that she keeps me grounded and tells me when I'm being a numpty. Thank you Teeks.

And to Bella, my faithful companion throughout the writing process, thank you for keeping my feet warm.

About Nina Mapson Bone

Everything Nina does is to create a world with more meaningful work. She is the Managing Director of Beaumont People, a recruitment and consulting firm that believes in placing people first. She is also President and Chair of the Recruitment, Consulting and Staffing Association of Australia and New Zealand, and the Chair of the Development Committee of the NORTH Foundation, a charity that supports medical research and patient care for the Northern Sydney Local Health District.

She has experienced first-hand the power of work to transform your life, and through her work in recruitment has seen time and again how, when engaged in meaningful work, every outcome at work improves for both the individual and the organisation. It is these observations that drive her to continue to help others in their own development of meaningful work.

www.ninamapsonbone.com.au

About Beaumont People

Established in 2001, Beaumont People specialises in delivering exceptional temporary and permanent recruitment solutions to diverse organisations across multiple industries. We recognise that organisations require different leadership at various stages of their life cycle, and in doing so embody our ideal of 'Placing People First'. Our success stems from combining integrity, excellence, ambition, collaboration, fun, and a dedication to meeting the needs of our candidates and clients.

Our services also extend to consulting and professional development, which includes our LEAD Mentoring and Professional Development Program; successfully run since 2017. We prioritise providing personalised service, building strong relationships and networks with our candidates and clients, and comprehending specific industry requirements.

www.beaumontpeople.com.au